I0817573

The Modern Japanese Garden

Contributions by:
Kengo Kuma
Mira Locher
Tim Richardson
Masuno Shunmyo

With 400 illustrations

The Modern Japanese Garden

Stephen
Mansfield

Foreword by Pico Iyer

CONTENTS

1

2

Japanese gardens function as everything from recreational spaces to art installations, even hermeneutic instruments used to divine the order of the cosmos. Both restricting and liberating, gardens delineate space, setting out permissible routes to travel through them. Although nature deviates within them, the sight lines in gardens obey the laws of geometry. Edith Wharton celebrated the skill required to blend these clean lines with untamed nature in her 1904 work *Italian Villas and Their Gardens*, when she wrote of the challenges faced in creating a 'subtle transition from the fixed and formal lines of art to the shifting and irregular lines of nature'. A sub-division of the visual arts, Japanese garden design embraces a natural, even cosmic order that is not always immediately apparent to the visitor. When we talk about the art of gardening, the emphasis is not on the garden as an art object, but on the process of designing and making a landscape, which, at its most accomplished, requires a high level of skill and artistry.

This book provides a brief introductory survey of the Japanese garden that celebrates the immense diversity of its designs, from animist-infused, prototypical stone arrangements placed in sacred groves, to extraordinary post-war innovations. Alongside colour and monochrome photography, it features a selection of blueprints and a number of guest essays from specialists in the fields of landscape design, garden aesthetics and architecture. There are no private residential gardens in the book. With a few exceptions, all the gardens featured are accessible to the public.

Although there is some consideration of flowers, including flowering shrubs and trees, Japanese gardens, unlike Western and tropical landscapes, are not primarily about colour. Where it exists, it tends to be site-specific: a peony, azalea or iris garden. Post-war gardens embrace more contemporary materials and are characterized by a reduction in colour range. Instances where flowers appear in significant quantities run the risk of lapsing into striking colour palettes more associated with flowerbeds and parterres found in parks.

The vast range of designs represented here provide an insight into the Japanese way of thinking and are a reminder that these are not simply gardens, but points of convergence for several art forms and cultural practices, from the tea ceremony to Zen meditation. To fully appreciate gardens requires a degree of cultural literacy that even many Japanese people may lack. The intention of this book is to equip the reader with something like a code-breaking manual to crack the enigma of the Japanese garden. Consider the Honpo-in Temple garden in Kyoto, for example. Flat stones encircle a tiny lotus pond, its form replicating the sun, which in Japanese can be read as *nichi*. Lotus in Japanese is *ren*. In this manner, the pond comes to represent the name Nichiren, an important priest and founder of a powerful Buddhist sect. When ideas like this are understood, concepts demystified, the pleasure of viewing the garden increases exponentially.

As we probe deeper into the astonishing world of the Japanese garden, reexamining form, grasping arcane symbolism and allegorical narrative, they begin to radiate a fresh, recharged vitality. Where we once saw surface, we now we see strata, complexity, profound depth.

1
Azalea bushes substitute for rocks in the dry landscape garden of Shoden-ji Temple in Kyoto.

2
A contemporary touch at the Abema Tower woodland in Tokyo.

Pico Iyer

8 Foreword

1

2

Shuffling through impassable crowds in Kyoto's celebrated bamboo forest this spring, I turned up a steep slope and stepped into a sanctuary of clarity, silence and calm. All around me were broad vistas – borrowed landscapes, you could say – amidst the narrow paths and stone lanterns of a classic Japanese garden. The grounds of Okochi Sanso were designed in the twentieth century, in response to the wishes of the movie star who owned the villa, yet here were the Buddha statues, the wooden Shinto shrine, you might find in sacred spaces all across the ancient capital.

Arriving for the first time in Japan tomorrow, a newcomer might well be struck by the ubiquitous Postmodern surfaces and imported clutter of our global times. But the longer I've stayed around Kyoto and Nara – more than thirty-seven years now – the more I've seen how much remains beautifully rooted in the old. This deeply illuminating and learned book reminds us of an 'eternal modern' in which even amidst concrete and glass – on top of a busy train station! – the twenty-first-century Japanese garden imparts much of the quiet and grace of a landscape designed 500 years ago.

Not long after I first set foot in Kyoto, I registered that you don't enter many a Japanese garden; it enters you. The stillness, the silence, the immaculate order make you feel as composed and motionless as the scene around you. It's a site less for seeing than for feeling, made not for walking, often, so much as sitting. A traditional Japanese garden is less like an immersive art experience than a still life; you step into the stillness and find a deeper life.

The revelation of this book is to show how the form is constantly evolving without ever entirely violating the assumptions of old. I love the bamboo gate and cherry blossoms of International House, partly because they sit within the most revved-up area in Tokyo, Roppongi; my wife and I often visit the Namba Parks shopping centre in Osaka because amidst its nine storeys of restaurants and boutiques are sudden explosions of manicured greenness. In the West we hear often about a connection to Buddhism (as in the enigmatic dry garden at Ryoan-ji), but it's a Shinto spirit that tells even my Japanese granddaughter that every last boulder, leaf and stream has a soul. They're living things – household deities of a kind – that deserve impeccable care as well as respect.

Five months ago, I chanced to meet the man who has been raking the sand at Tofuku-ji in Kyoto for thirty-five years. As Takao Noriyuki taught me how to evoke streams and hills through swirls and ridges, he kept saying, gently, 'Don't think of anything. Just let the moment guide you.' Tofuku-ji is celebrated as one of the five 'Zen mountains' of Japan, a huge temple that has presided over southeastern Kyoto for 800 years. But its gardens, quite wonderfully, arrived only in 1939, as if to remind us that meditation – and reality – never grow old.

Step off jampacked Shijo Street in central Kyoto next week and climb to the top floor of the Kahitsukan Museum: there, in a tiny space, you'll find the sudden grace of tree and light that's pictured here. The wisdom of Japan is to see that the old never grows outdated; the beauty of Japan is to keep finding fresh imaginative ways of making it eternally new.

1
An ancient Buddhist relief incised into a rock in Kyoto's Hakusasonso Garden.

2
The virtues of tradition. Powdered green tea at Hosen-in, a temple in Ohara.

Stephen Mansfield

10 Introduction: Prototypes and Forms

1

'Driven by the urge to make the invisible, mysterious forces of nature tangible, man saw a singular substance stand out in the gloom of primeval nature – a solid, immovable rock.'

— Tange Kenzo[1]

11

In the search for the origins of the Japanese garden, we have to return in time to an animist world of mountains, riverbeds and forest glades. Unlike Francis Bacon, who claimed, 'God Almighty first planted a garden',[2] the ancient Japanese had to contend not with a single god, a monotheistic authority, but with a swarm of innumerable deities.

Simple arrangements of stones were placed by men and women in woodlands and on pebbly clearings beside waterfalls and rivers, in deference to the gods, perhaps even with a touch of fear for the calamities that could ensue if the correct observances were not made. In a world devoid of temples, shrines or religious texts, nature provided a stage on which rocks, trees, mountain peaks and purling brooks, substituting as high altars, acted as vectors through which the gods connected with man. These clearings, boundary zones created between this world and the next, the divine and human, were known as *kekkai*. Sacred precincts strewn with pebbles, white sand or gravel, in which ritual ablutions were performed, were named *shiki no himorogi*.

Large boulders called *iwakura* (spirit rocks) and *iwasaki* (stone seats) were placed in spaces conducive to worship and benevolent co-existence. *Yu-niwa* and *sa-niwa* were purified zones meant for prayer, *kami-ike*, sacred ponds. Other forms of demarcated space included sacred stone circles and *iwa-saka*, twin rocks forming a narrow passage that evoked an image of female genitalia. Purified spaces were indicated by sacred stones and trees, the forms encircled with rice-fibre ropes called *shimenawa*. During devotional rituals in these settings, nature was no longer mute or alien, but a powerfully animate, articulate force.

Making an enclosure, establishing boundaries, marks the beginning of a garden. A convincing argument could be made that these ritual spaces, the abode of *kami* (gods), constituted the outlines of a recognizable garden, a prototypical dry landscape, prefiguring the later centrality of rocks in the Japanese garden. Links with these open enclosures can be traced to Shinto shrines today, with their cordoned-off pebble beds, sand cones known as *tatesuna* and sacred plants, like *sakaki* (*Cleyera japonica*). While retaining its strong animistic character, Shinto, Japan's native religion, articulated these ideas, providing a vocabulary that aligned a primitive belief system with theology.

In opposition to other, more perishable features in nature, rock represented permanence, immutability. Humans were regarded as temporal, only their spirits eternal. Rocks were, therefore, associated with the deceased, repositories where the spirits could return. In Shinto thinking, objects of veneration, ranging from a pebble to a towering peak, are the habitat of *amakudaru kami*, spirit forms that descend from above, while *torai kami* enter the terrestrial world from the sea. Shinto, a syncretic faith rooted in nature worship, divination, fertility cults and shamanism, holds that the gods are immanent in nature, co-existing symbiotically with its inherent forces. There is a strong sense that a life within nature, and a respect for its indwelling powers, is synonymous with co-existing with the gods. Trees, in this system of thinking, functioned as intermediaries with the *kami*, obviating the necessity for man-made structures. The forest served as a shrine without buildings. Where the Japanese garden most deviates from Western landscaping is in its borrowings from animism and its links to native Shintoism and later importations of Taoist and Buddhist principles. In this syncretic Japanese cosmology, rocks and organic matter are not inanimate objects, but receptors for the cosmic and telluric energy present in the universe.

Buddhism purportedly entered Japan in 552 CE. The catalyst for its emergence appears to have been a gift of sutras and religious images from the king of Paekche (present-day Korea). Chinese influences, along with the appropriation of Buddhist and geomantic principles, were evident in Japanese gardens created from the sixth century onwards. Developing along the inland portions of the Yellow River, Chinese garden culture had an immeasurable impact on early Japanese garden forms.

With the introduction of Buddhism came a cosmology drawn from Indian-derived teachings. According to this vision of the universe, a huge mountain known as Mount Meru stood at the centre of the world. Its motif, known in Japanese as Shumisen, is often seen in gardens as a single upright stone supported by a concentric arrangement of secondary rocks. When a Japanese emissary returned home in 607 CE with a detailed account of Chinese garden design methods, Empress Suiko had a garden designed that was inspired by the mythic peak.

1
A sacred *iwakura* rock at Achi Shrine in Kurashiki. The rock is strung with a sacred *shimenawa* rope made from twisted dried rice straw.

2

3

Dating from the eighth-century Nara period (710–94), the excavated and reconstructed To-in Teien (East Palace Garden), part of Nara's Heijo Palace Complex, is a study in the considered application of geomancy, and its effects on landforms. A curvaceous pebble beach, a *suhama*, prefigures later representations of paradise, while the vermilion pavilion and bridges are similar in colour to Shinto shrines. Drawing on Chinese mythology, the pond contained a number of small islands. A *kyokusui*, a meandering stream, marks the spot where banquets were held. Reflecting Chinese and Japanese horticultural tastes, the renovated grounds have been planted with camellia, willow, plum and cypress.

By the Heian period (794–1185), gardens had already begun to incorporate more complex rock groupings, plant arrangements and island groupings. An outcrop of rocks and pine trees might be a visualization of the sandbar of Ama-no-Hashidate in the west of Japan, or the islands of Matsushima to the northeast; a tortoise-shaped island represented longevity and the mythical isles of the Chinese Immortals. A particular stone might be named Fudo-myoo, after the Buddhist divinity of fire; other arrangements evoked desolate mountain ranges and shorelines. In this way, primordial sculptural forms were imbued with sophisticated concepts whose provenance was both cultural and spiritual.

Heian-era homes of the nobility were called *shinden-zukuri*, the name deriving from the residence's south-facing hall. The structures featured a series of covered passages connecting the main buildings and pavilions, the decks acting as viewing platforms onto small gardens. The act of compression required to contain landscapes within the framework of the residence would influence the development of the Japanese garden. These modest, interspatial arrangements were planted with shrubs, small trees and seasonal flowers containing literary connections familiar to poetry-loving courtiers. Geomancy dictated that a stream flow beneath the buildings in a northeast to south direction, where a pond was auspiciously located. Small islands were connected by red-lacquered Chinese-style bridges. These pond gardens, augmented in a picturesque style with artificial hills and pathways, were called *tsukiyama-teien*. Nara and Heian period gardens are characterized by a mixture of reverence and playfulness. *Shirasu*, white sand courts, were for conducting ceremonies beside garden ponds used to entertain guests, who, accompanied by music, would board *ryuto-gekishu* pleasure crafts, decorated with the figureheads of dragons and a *geki*, a mythological bird of Chinese origin.

The mysteries of the Japanese garden were jealously guarded among a small and exclusive fraternity of professionals, secret manuals passed among the initiated like sacred parchments. The *Sakutei-ki*, a detailed garden manual written in the eleventh century by Tachibana no Toshitsuna, describes both the rules for constructing Chinese-style gardens and a more intuitive way of creating landscapes in tune with emerging Japanese tastes. The book concerns itself with geomancy, the correct setting of stones, the circulation of water and the felicitous disposition of land features. The manual begins with the opening line, 'Obey the request of the stone.' In a world where every object in nature was animate, guidance on placement was sought from individual rocks. Compared to the pragmatic gardening manuals found in Western countries, the *Sakutei-ki* is a rather philosophical work, invoking cosmological models and principles ranging from feng shui to *gogyo*, the theory of the five elements. The principles of the manual are less about replicating nature than studying it and finding methods to harmoniously correspond garden design to topography. Motsu-ji, a Heian-era garden in Hiraizumi, is the only remaining almost completely intact garden designed according to the principles of the *Sakutei-ki*.

By the end of the Heian period, an era characterized by paradise gardens representing the Buddhist Pure Land, Japan, the ever-attentive student, had become the master of its own landscape forms. Similarities in garden design would widen, dilute and eventually dissolve as indigenous Japanese landscape ideas and new standards emerged, then predominated.

The resplendent grounds and precious Buddhist sculptures of the Pure Land gardens and temples were superseded by the more introspective, non-material aspirations of the stone garden. The principal schemata of the Japanese garden have always been its arrangements of rocks, to the extent that in this period there was no word for gardening; the process was described instead as *ishi wo taten koto*, 'the practice of setting stones'. Conferring with their *ishigokoro*, or inner heart, priests engaged in collaborative decisions with the spirits of natural matter when considering rock placement. Tasked with applying geomantic principles aimed at averting misfortune, misaligning even a single stone could alter the Earth's movement, muddle the desirable routes and circulatory paths of *ki*, the life force, and bring down misfortune and sickness on the heads of garden owners. It's likely that the priests who applied themselves to making gardens did so without consciously thinking of themselves as gardeners per se. In the role of channelling mediums, gardeners even today invoke the phrase *ishi no kowan ni shitagahite*, meaning, 'When setting garden stones, listen to the wishes of the stone.'

A second wave of Chinese culture, philosophy and aesthetics arrived in the twelfth, thirteenth and fourteenth centuries, notable among the influences the Chan sect of Chinese Buddhism. 'Zen' in the Japanese reading of the word, with its emphasis on discipline and self-reliance, had immense appeal to the warrior class of the Kamakura period (1185–1333). Rocks came to be seen as symbols of Zen, or as allegorical elements in Buddhist narrative. Symbolism could be used not only to add depth and erudition to gardens, but, through an unfolding of associations, to expand the spatial aspects of the mind. Rocks in early Japanese theophany were no longer anonymous masses of sedimentary or igneous matter, but vectors of faith and enlightenment. Rinzai Zen monk Muso Soseki (1275–1351) was an early proponent of the idea of stripping gardens down to essential elements. Under the influence of designers like Muso, sacred stones were once again imbued with the numinous, but this time as repositories for Buddha nature. This subtractive, deifying process led to the advent of the dry landscape garden.

The Zen propensity for symbolism and paradox resulted in other intriguing antinomies. One example is the interpretation of water in lithic gardens. The metaphysical nature of the stone garden allows us to accept the existence of features like the dry waterfall, an apparent contradiction in terms. Raked sand and gravel are perceived as waves. Conspiring with the illusion, we refrain from stepping onto the sand, as if it were actual water. According to art historian Yoshinaga Yoshinobu, metaphorical water may surpass reality: 'The garden is an attempt to represent the innermost essence of water, without actually using water, and to represent it as that even more profoundly than would be possible with real water.'[3]

With the advent of the Muromachi era (1333–1573), spacious residences with relatively small, compressed gardens installed viewing decks that encouraged contemplation of the stone garden rather than physical engagement. In contrast to the privileged world of the Heian-era nobility, a more sombre warrior-class ethic began to emerge. Based on simplicity and frugality, the aesthetic of *yugen*, denoting profound, mystic beauty, influenced the creation of austere gardens. The energizing emptiness created by large, unpainted areas of canvases, known as *yohaku-no-bi*, prioritizing absence over the present, the manifest, was applied to the dry landscape garden, with its expanses of sand and gravel. These sparse landscapes co-opted the Zen concept of *mu*, nothingness, or emptiness, and the teaching that the phenomenal world is an illusion. Japanese gardeners have always been aware of the two key concepts of Chinese-derived cosmology and philosophy: plenitude and void. Emptiness, space stripped of content, however, is not perceived as sterile. Architectural historian Yagasaki Zentaro wrote, 'Nothingness in Buddhism is not seen as an end, but as a space that sets things in motion.'[4] Because space and time are not regarded as independent matter in Japan, the empty and the replete are not considered separate entities, but reciprocally energizing, enjoined forces. In this formulation, structure and empty space are interdependent.

2
Misogi, Shinto water purification rituals, are often performed beneath waterfalls, like this one near Toba.

3
Ritual changing of *shimenawa* sacred rope. Meoto Iwa (Wedded Rocks), Futami.

4
To-in Garden. Restored Nara-era (710–94) garden in Nara.

4

Opulence and frugality continued to co-exist in the Middle Ages, represented in architecture by the castle and teahouse, the muscular culture of the warrior class contrasting with the restrained aesthetics of the tea ceremony. The rustic teahouse, modelled after the *soan*, a grass-roofed hut, was approached through a small *cha-niwa* (tea garden) of equally modest proportions. Under Sen no Rikyu (1522–1591), the tea ceremony was refined into a form known as *wabi-cha*, the Way of Tea, which involved an appreciation of imperfection that redefined the Japanese sense of beauty. Rikyu, instrumental in defining the tea ceremony as a spiritual exercise, dubbed these gardens *roji*, meaning the 'dewy way', a word that also refers to a Buddhist sutra depicting a place where souls are reborn. The *roji* represented a new form of Japanese gardening art that aspired to elegant rusticity.

As guests walk down the freshly sprinkled path of the tea garden, they undergo a journey, a passage from the outer world, with all its impurities, to a room dedicated to refined introspection. This transition involves a willing dissociation that is aided by a non-distractive backdrop of graduated greenery, what the Chinese, referring to moss, called 'liquid jade'. Uneven stepping stones are integral to the tea garden. Because of their irregularity, guests are obliged to pay attention to the path. This also reduces the speed of movement through the grounds, inducing a more studied consideration of the garden. Often compared to an inner sanctuary, the tea garden and its central structure, the teahouse, are aligned according to the principle of *oku*, the limiting of immediate vision through methods of envelopment. The resulting effect is a garden that resembles a hermitage situated deep within the mountains. In urban areas, such gardens are referred to as *shichu no in*, hidden sites within the city.

5

Kyoto, with its hills, woodland and ready supply of rocks, gravel and water, was the natural location for the cultivation of large estate gardens connected to the imperial family. Shugaku-in Imperial Villa and Katsura Rikyu Imperial Villa, gardens with skilfully framed perspectives, are fine examples of the genre. Like the more private, introspective tea garden, a countertrend to the luxurious acreages of imperial gardens materialized in the severely scaled-down courtyard garden. There was a clear connection between the two design types, as garden historian Ito Teiji asserts: 'The model for the urban courtyard garden was the tea garden.'[5] The smallest and most secluded form, surrounded on four sides by residential rooms, the *tsubo niwa* requires, at its most minimal, little more than one or two stones, a gravel surface and a few plantings. A bucolic and aesthetically pleasing spot at the centre of a residence, the design also acts as a light well, bringing air and natural illumination into the centre of confined, shaded homes. There is more flexibility in the *naka-niwa*, another version of the courtyard garden. The sumptuous expanses of moss and trees within the courtyard garden of the Tamogawa Imperial Villa in Nikko are a good example. Although tiny courtyard gardens may host seasonal efflorescence like winter camellia and *tsuwabuke* (spotted leopard plant), they invariably revert to simpler motifs consisting of stone ornamentation and greenery. Air wells conveying rain and shafts of sunlight keep the gardens moist. Those where light rarely penetrates may acquire the faint dampness of a neglected graveyard or sepulchre.

The closest surviving forms to the Heian-period paradise gardens were Edo-period (1600–1868) stroll gardens. During this era, in which the Tokugawa regime oversaw over two and a half centuries of relative peace and stability, achieved through a policy of national self-isolation, the authorities brooked little dissent. Discouraged from spending funds on enlarging their military arsenals, warriors and members of the nobility, known as *daimyo*, chose instead to pursue leisure activities of a cultural nature. This disabling of an entire martial class resulted in wealth being rechannelled, with the aristocracy becoming avid collectors of art, rare tea bowls, brocades and damask. The nobility amused themselves constructing large, ambitious gardens. Many of these landscapes were representational, cleverly mirroring concepts and settings, both real and imaginary, found in Chinese and Japanese history and literature. This entitled class were well read and educated, familiar with the Japanese and Chinese classics, Confucian doctrine and the complexities of esoteric Buddhism.

The *kaiyushiki-teien*, or stroll garden, is a genre that attempts to represent natural, cultural, scenic and historical features in a visual digest designed to stimulate and enthral guests. Despite injunctions to modesty, some of these *daimyo* gardens were enormous and costly undertakings. The stroll garden provided a setting for members of the nobility and guests to meander at their leisure past a set of *mises-en-scène*, which might include the celebrated causeway transecting Hangzhou's West Lake in China, the islands of Japan's Inland Sea, the coast at Tamatsushima in Kii Province, Mount Lu in Jiangxi Province or scenes from the fifty-three stages of the old Tokaido highway. Visitors followed a route that featured *meisho*, or 'famous sights'. These landscape compendiums obviated the need

6

7

to undertake arduous journeys over mountain passes on foot, on horseback or by boat, which might involve months away from home. Koraku-en, a garden in Okayama city, is a fine example of the form, incorporating an artificial thicket with miniature valleys, mountains and waterfalls that are said to be modelled on scenery along the ancient Kiso Road. Okayama Castle, just beyond the perimeters of the garden, forms part of a *shakkei*, or 'borrowed view', an optical effect used to expand space and create deeper perspective, while integrating natural and architectural features beyond the garden's parameters.

Edo-era gardeners, unknowingly acknowledging English landscape designer William Kent's dictum, 'Nature abhors a straight line', welcomed irregularity in the form of slopes and uneven contouring. Where they were absent, sinuous, undulating landscapes were created. The earth from excavated ponds was used to erect hillocks and mounds in an effort to replicate a natural, graduated topography. In some instances, the natural environs needed little alteration. According to a period garden commentary called *Koraku-en kiji*, when creating Koishikawa Koraku-en, Tokyo's oldest *daimyo* garden, the designer Sahei Tokudaiji was at pains to 'build the garden without felling old trees or altering the contours of the land, in the belief that things were better left in their natural state'.[6] The garden was the first example of the subsequently much emulated design concept known as *chikei ni yorite*, meaning to follow and adapt to an existing landscape.

Entering these excursion gardens, we follow a predetermined route along paths where only partial views are provided. Our vision of the garden and its scale is manipulated by altered perspective. Garden elements play an important role in this process. If rocks and trees placed in the foreground are larger than their counterparts in the background, for example, the designer has achieved an illusion of depth. In another technique, known as *miegakure* (hide-and-reveal), common to Japanese stroll gardens, trees, plantings, artificial hills and fences are used in such a way that only sections of the garden can be seen at any given moment. By providing a sequential narrative, the *kaiyushiki-teien* created multiple perspectives on a single, cohesive landscape, viewed within a controlled visual frame.

The Japanese have long excelled at managed miniaturization, though, properly speaking, the process in stroll garden design is closer to representation and scale manipulation, the results often more playful than solemn. Noting that, at an early stage in Japan's creation of a cultural identity, 'the avatar of Walt Disney was alive and well', the writer Donald Richie cited the example of Rikugi-en, a prominent Edo-era stroll garden. Here, he noted, 'in one place, arranged somewhat like a miniature golf course, are all of the 88 classical sites, all tiny, and all with noticeboards explaining the Chinese or Japanese association'.[7] Informal pictorial gardens, re-scaling cultural sights in the manner of the *jardin anglo-chinois*, apply picturesque or poetic principles to create dioramas. Like the Augustan gardens of eighteenth-century England, with their borrowed Doric and Corinthian elements, the stroll garden was a compendium of highly personalized tastes, of reductive, real and mythological landscapes and iconic sights, architectural structures, Buddhist sculpture and stone adornments.

Karikomi (topiary) appeared at this time, the meticulously clipped bushes and evergreens representing everything from treasure ships to billowing clouds. Setting aside large areas for topiary provides visual variety through the rhythmic repetition of species, shrubs and bushes across sight lines placed at differing depths throughout gardens.

The era witnessed an efflorescence of townspeople-driven culture. The shift from fine art and Noh drama to the feisty, plebeian theatre of Kabuki and the mass production of woodblock prints depicting famous sights, actors and courtesans from the pleasure quarters paralleled major economic shifts. As the warrior class became increasingly strapped, the merchant class gradually acquired wealth and began to patronize the popular new arts. In order

5
Located in the grounds of the Homma Museum of Art in Sakata, this landscape is a fine example of a privately owned stroll garden.

6
Courtyard garden, Northern Culture Museum, Konan ward, Niigata.

7
Tea garden, Daiho-in, Kyoto.

8
Topiary. From *Tsukiyama Teizoden* (*Building Mountains and Making Gardens*), Edo-era garden manual.

9
The billowing topiary at Raikyu-ji Temple in Bitchu-Takahashi is the work of the influential designer Enshu Kobori (1579–1647).

8

9

to keep up appearances and save face, the ruling class would affect a pretence of affluence, the merchant class one of penury. Although horticulture flourished among the lower orders, garden design on a grand, conceptual scale remained the preserve of the nobility.

The gardens of the feudal lords were not open to the general public, who began to rely for design ideas and guidance on woodblock-printed and illustrated garden manuals and treatises, circulated, often in pirated form, among an increasingly literate public. Handmade sample catalogues were distributed by travelling book lenders. Illustrated books on gardening were now accessible to everyone. The popular and relatively inexpensive *Tsukiyama Teizoden* (*Building Mountains and Making Gardens*), published in 1735, is an example of an illustrated text providing a realistic overview of gardening methods.

By the late Edo period, the literary allusions and meanings connected to garden features diminished, as landscaping became more mannerist and tastes degraded, gardens filling with novelty elements, like outdoor furnishings and miniaturized architectural follies aimed at creating a wonderland, a gated Arcadia.

As outside pressure mounted on Japan to open up to trade with the West, opposition to the Tokugawa regime reached critical mass. Disorder manifested in a series of political assassinations, intrigues, coups, social turmoil, the rise of millenarian cults and a revival of emperor worship, with the forces of the shogun pitted against the reformist, anti-feudal faction. Under the new order, members of a now outdated samurai class loyal to the deposed shogun were ruined, without property or stipends. In the vacuum between the dissolution of the old feudal system and the ascendance of a new order, lawlessness and chaos thrived. Thieves occupied the grand mansions of the *daimyo*. The homeless lurked on the edges of these great estates, occasionally sleeping in their dark thickets. Malcontent, disputatious *ronin* (masterless samurai), abusive, armed and dangerous, roamed through untended gardens.

With the abolition of the feudal system and the restoration of the emperor in the new Meiji era (1868–1912), the country's *daimyo* gardens, especially those in Edo, now renamed Tokyo, the 'eastern capital', faced near extinction. For all its bombastic, self-promoting talk of *bunmei kaika* (civilization and enlightenment), the new order showed a stunning disregard for the value of landscape gardening, one of the nation's foremost cultural achievements.

The newly installed government set about levelling properties and gardens, replacing them with tea and mulberry fields. Appropriated by the authorities as military facilities, centres for the promotion of industry or sites for foreign embassies, many of the grandest *daimyo* gardens were razed to the ground. Even the prototypical Koishikawa Koraku-en had part of its grounds requisitioned as a munitions factory. The garden historian Keijiro Ozawa, though a fervent proponent of Meiji-era modernization, was appalled by the desecration of garden culture. On a visit to Koraku-en, he observed, 'Since the munitions plant was built here, chimney-stacks have been belching more smoke every year, causing many of the trees to wither from the top until they eventually die.'[8] In the fever for advancement, to promote industry and exports, to increase foreign currency reserves, only a handful of *daimyo* gardens would survive.

The Nursery City

The British botanist Robert Fortune (1812–1880), visiting Japan in the early 1860s, was struck by how advanced the interest in horticulture was among all social classes. In his book *A Narrative of a Journey to the Capitals of Japan and China*, he noted the 'flower-loving national character', the level of gardening culture and the extent to which it had been diffused among common people.

As the population of Edo (Tokyo) expanded, creating tightly quartered blocks in the poorer, inner districts, airless warrens of narrow alleys and compressed communal space, so thankfully, did its greenery. In an age of aristocratic gardens and samurai estates, there were also shrine and temple compounds where groves of trees stood, and natural riverbanks where wild grasses, herbs and flowers gained purchase.

The townspeople of Edo cherished potted plants, placing them along the walls and open culverts of their narrow backstreet homes. Pinched frontages provided just enough space for a row of azaleas, calabashes, morning glory and *kudzu* vines, brightening up otherwise dismal passageways. Horticulture thrived in a city where flowers and greenery remained an important part of daily life. Lower-ranking *gokenin*, though less well paid than other shogunal retainers, maintained small gardens, setting aside land for the commercial cultivation of flowers and saplings. Interacting with nurserymen and tradespeople, they played a key role in the dissemination of gardening techniques and horticulture.

Advances in printing technology made it possible to publish garden-related books and manuals. This had been done at an early stage by Ito Ihei, a gardener in the Somei district of Edo, when he published his *Kadan Jikinsho*, a manual on gardening, but a huge spur to popularizing horticulture came in the Meiwa era (1764–72) with the availability of polychrome *ukiyo-e* woodblock prints. Here, we see courtesans admiring irises in small, fenced plots within the confines of the Yoshiwara pleasure district, crowds enjoying the spring cherry blossoms in Mukojima and townspeople stopping at street corners to inspect New Year pine decorations. Other prints show attendees at azalea and chrysanthemum festivals. A woodblock print by the artist Hasegawa Settan depicts a lively mix of samurai, monks, geisha and commoners thronging a plant fair at Yakushi-in temple in Kayabacho, where interest is added to familiar species like wisteria and bamboo with the inclusion of exotic imports like cactus, cycads and orchids. Excursions to see plum and cherry trees planted in temple and shrine precincts or along water courses became popular. Thanks to the tree-planting policy of the eighth shogun, Tokugawa Yoshimune, the number of scenic spots for cherry blossom viewing increased, especially along river embankments. Floriculture even manifested itself on the Kabuki stage, where potted plants were used as props. Edo became known throughout Japan as 'the city of flowers'.

The construction of mansions inhabited by a noble class of *daimyo* lords saw the arrival of large numbers of gardeners, tasked with designing and maintaining these spacious estates. As an interest in gardening spread to the lower orders and the demand for plants rose, many gardeners became independent nurserymen, running their own horticultural enterprises and developing new species. The popularity of excursions among the townspeople to places of seasonal scenic beauty encouraged commercial

1

1
Rikugi-en. Azalea-lined steps ascend to the Fujishiro Toge, the highest artificial hill in the garden.

2

3

4

2
Azalea bushes add a welcome dash of colour to gardens and parks throughout Japan in late April and May.

3
A splendid collision of lilac wisteria and azaleas at the Ashikaga Flower Park in Tochigi Prefecture.

4
Rows of azaleas harmonize perfectly with a tunnel of vermilion *tori* gates at the Nezu Shrine in Tokyo.

5

gardeners to open up their yards to the public. In this manner, trained artisans working for the nobility became merchants, altering the socio-economic character of the city. Plants became commodities that people thirsted for.

Japanese scholars believed that winter was a time for quiet pleasures, contemplation and study, a season when yang currents, still strong in late autumn, would begin to fade, making way for the softer, more pliable yin forces. Winter is the most introspective season for Japanese flora, but its gardens are rarely bereft of colour. There are evergreens, broad-leaf plants and even the occasional bloom. This is the season for the glossy red berries of the *senryo*, a shrub whose name means 'a thousand gold pieces'. Another hardy evergreen shrub, *jinchoge* (winter daphne), releases an intoxicating fragrance into the air in late February. The floral highlights of the season would have to include the narcissus, January's fragrant plum blossoms and the deep red and pink blooms of winter camellia. Luxuriant displays of pink, red and white peonies appeared in Edo temple gardens and parks at this time of year, creating another quintessentially Japanese scene. Introduced from China in the eighth century, the flower has inspired poets, playwrights, tattoo artists, woodblock printers, kimono designers and painters, the latter covering sliding doors and folding screens with their brilliance.

Native species of pink, white and magenta azaleas and ornamentals, a signature spring flower, along with cherry and wisteria, were discovered to be especially well suited to the climate and soil of the city. Along with early summer rainy-season hydrangeas and irises, the morning glory has long been synonymous with the life of the city. The fad for the flower among the townspeople was matched by a more serious quest among temple priests and samurai with skills in floriculture to develop cultivars that could be entered into competitions. A passion for the morning glory, visible in many prints from this period, was even responsible for a degree of social levelling. Despite their differences in rank, Tomejiro Yamazaki, a nurseryman, and Lord Naotaka Nabeshima developed a friendly rivalry and collaboration.

Every season has its blooms, and autumn, with its pampas grass, buckwheat flowers, spider lily and the fragrant orange osmanthus, is no exception. The so-called Seven Flowers of Autumn, portrayed in screen paintings, lacquerware and kimono designs, include *hagi* (bush clover), often included in formal gardens to give them a rustic, natural touch. The other flowers in the grouping are the *kikyo* (bell flower), *fujibakama* (Japanese boneset), *ominaeshi* (patrinia), *nadeshiko* (fringed pink flower), *kudzu* and *susuki* (Japanese silver grass).

The Edo era is noted as being a time of cultural efflorescence in the arts, supported by professionals and enthusiasts from every social rank, but also a period when floriculture attained an extraordinary level of connoisseurship.

6

5
An Edo-period courtesan attending to her chrysanthemums.

6
Edo-era *ukiyo-e* prints made for children, who would learn about flowers and plants by cutting out the shapes.

7

8

9

7
A traditional oiled umbrella adds a decorative touch to the more formal striations of hedge, bamboo and autumn leaves.

8
The combination of leafy, sun-dappled canopy, water and flowering azaleas create the illusion of an earthly paradise at Toji-in, a temple garden in west Kyoto.

9
Wisteria pendants suspended from a pergola at the Kameido Tenjin Shrine in eastern Tokyo.

10
A high-ranking courtesan attending one of Edo's many flower fairs, this one during the plum season.

10

21

1

Part 1

Gardens of the Entrepreneurs: 1900–45

1 ←
A view across the main pond at Soraku-en in Kobe, of a rustic teahouse.
2
A large courtyard garden in the Tamozawa Imperial Villa in Nikko, a forested area known for its lush beds of moss.

25

Visitors to the Japanese pavilions of the 1900 Exposition Universelle in Paris would have encountered a simulacrum of the Japanese garden that was already out of date, if it ever existed at all. The Japan-British Exhibition, held in London's White City district in 1910, offered a similarly misleading digest. Judging from photogravures and postcards celebrating the event, its Garden of the Floating Island was a rather cluttered affair, a jam of clumsy lines of stone placements akin to an English rockery, randomly placed stone lanterns and pagodas, ill-sorted tree and bush plantings and a Japanese-style temple, adjacent to an ornate bridge of Chinese stylistic provenance. The result is an oddly Orientalized, hastily botched composition. Despite the artless landscaping at some of these international exhibitions and others like them in North America, the displays did nothing to quell the fashion among Westerners for *Japonaiserie* gardens.

With the advent of the Meiji period (1868–1912), the association of the stroll garden with *meisho*, the recreation of famous sites or fictive scenery from literature, Buddhism and mythology, reorientated towards Western concepts of landscape and nature. One influence behind this was the shift away from Japanese *sansuiga* (mountain and water painting) to *fukeiga* (landscape painting). The trend was accelerated by the influence of Japanese writers and artists familiar with British cultural figures known for their reinterpretations of the natural world, among them the writer John Ruskin, with his philosophy of 'truth to nature', and the painter John Turner. A more objectified Western view of nature was expressed in Roka Tokutomi's (1868–1927) book *Shizen to Jinsei* (Nature and Life), published in 1900.

The shift from symbolism and representation in garden design to a non-symbolic style of naturalism is embodied in the Kyoto garden of Murin-an. Although schooled in traditional landscape methods, its designer, Ogawa Jihei (1860–1933), became known for more naturalistic layouts corresponding to the principles and tastes of English landscape gardens. Murin-an was commissioned by Arimoto Yamagata, a field marshal who would later become the prime minister of a clannish, quasi-feudalistic cabinet. He seems an unlikely patron of gardens, but he appears to have possessed considerable discernment, taking a keen interest in the designs. The spirit of modern openness that permeates Murin-an owes much to his ideas and experiences, as he had travelled extensively in Europe and the United States. In London, Yamagata saw numerous residential garden squares with extensive lawns and diverse tree plantings, but was also exposed to public spaces, including St James' Park, which had been remodelled in 1827 by John Nash, from a romantic garden into a more naturalistic landscape with expansive lawns and a lake.

In Ogawa, a master gardener fully confident of his own skills, Yamagata seems to have met his match. One telling exchange has him trying to impose his ideas on Ogawa, only to be told, 'When it comes to manoeuvring armies, Mr Yamagata, you are the undisputed leader in Japan, but when it comes to making a garden, leave that to me.'[1] Ogawa's temerity in scolding his patron seems to have worked, and henceforth he was given a free hand, although it is likely that the template for the garden was Yamagata's, the results a collaboration of converging taste. Ogawa's designs may strike the casual observer as traditional, but his innovative use of water, seen in the group of gardens he went on to create in the residential portions of the Nanzen-ji district of eastern Kyoto, drawing water from the Lake Biwa Canal, favour naturalism over symbolism, signalling a significant shift towards the modern Japanese garden of the period.

Themes and symbolism, important features of older gardens, were largely absent from the landscape designs of the Meiji period onwards, which saw a shift towards the personal tastes of the wealthy clients who commissioned them. Styles of gardening synonymous with the preceding Edo era were either abandoned or modified. The absence of outstanding tea masters meant that tea gardens, suffering a lack of innovation, were reduced to simplistic replications of former styles. Imitations of Western landscape design drew local inspiration from the forests and streams surrounding big cities and the flora of Japan's alpine regions. The Meiji government, eager to invest in public landscaping, funded a number of Western-style parks. With the draconian travel restrictions of the security-obsessed Edo era effectively lifted, the citizenry now enjoyed greater mobility and exposure to varied landscape forms, hitherto only accessible in books, paintings and woodblock prints of dubious visual authenticity.

The restitution of the emperor and the end of feudalism in the Meiji era are often seen as predominantly political and social changes, but these shifts also had an unexpected impact on garden design. As the general public's interest in traditional gardens dwindled, landscape masterpieces were allowed to decay. Abruptly considered out of date, rustic garden ornaments and beautifully formed rocks were auctioned off. As author

Alex Kerr wrote of the period, 'Once the world of old Japan had vanished, it was time to recycle the fragments.'[2] Garden clients were now of a different order. Instead of shoguns, head priests, court aristocracy and feudal lords, the new patrons of gardens were government officials, plutocrats and businessmen, an empowered nouveau riche, a bourgeois class with an interest in Western styles of gardening based on a leisurely enjoyment of space. Initially, these designs simply replicated the feudal models of the Edo era, but with more exposure to the schools of naturalism that were especially popular in England, landscapes began to fuse formalism with a fresh interest in plants and lawns. A new use was found for stones in Meiji gardens, less for their symbolic or iconic value than as design accents.

Much of the land once owned by *daimyo* passed into the hands of this affluent new Meiji elite. Many of these gardens, like the grounds of the current Australian embassy in Tokyo, where one former baron kept aviaries, had secret doors installed in wardrobes leading to the boudoirs of in-house concubines and had telephones mysteriously placed amidst ferns and shrubbery, are long gone.

To the unschooled eye, many of the surviving designs may look quite traditional. Closer examination reveals some notable differences. More introspective, they represent private domains of ownership and privilege. Lawns with woodland borders were laid and purling streams dug, to create the feeling of an English parkland. The more muscular, assertive ornamentation of the period represented a growing confidence. The presence of large stone lanterns and recycled decorative elements like millstones and stone pillar pedestals, as well as the placement of oversized *kutsu-nugi-ishi* (shoe-removing stones), suggest hubris, the acquisition of objects as status symbols. Large *tachi-chozubachi* standing water basins, for example, introduced into gardens in the sixteenth century, became popular revival objects. Scale and height accorded with the social status of the people using them. Members of the aristocracy tended to stand up straight when washing their hands, commoners to stoop. Members of the lower ranks, therefore, used suitably lower basins.

3

Despite the beauty of many of these gardens, they continued to function as indicators of conspicuous wealth and consumption, a measure of financial standing and influence. With garden landscaping no longer regarded as an art, and with Western garden and park designs coming to the fore, private estates turned away from Japanese formalism. Under this new naturalism, evergreens were thinned; the predominant trees of this period were young, open plantings of deciduous specimens. Low woody plants were grown on the forest floors of gardens. Oaks and maples helped to create a woodland ambience, with skilful planting concealing the boundaries of the garden, suggesting more space than actually existed.

Detractors of the new style suggested that the unlimited funds of this new entrepreneurial class led to a decline in aesthetic taste and a favouring of the novel and ostentatious. Other critics pointed out that, because some gardens eschewed the use of existing landscape forms, the results were a kind of applied or invented naturalism. Old farmhouses, suitable settings for the tea ceremony, for example, were sometimes bought and then reconstructed in gardens, the scale of the reassembled structures far eclipsing the traditional, deliberately modest tea hut, with its suggestion of tasteful frugality. As well as the influence of English naturalism, ecological movements were flourishing in Germany and the Netherlands, and ideas from the Arts and Crafts schools were beginning to gain attention in Japan.

4

3
Tofuku-ji. Geometrically pruned hedges contrast with sinuous curves.

4
A segment of the Yamamoto-tei garden, commissioned by a wealthy manufacturer of camera components. The *yuki-tsuri* frames are to protect trees from heavy snowfall.

5 →
Soraku-en. A centuries-old boathouse, once used to entertain guests.

6
Tofuku-ji. Powerful rock clusters like this typify Shigemori Mirei's work.
7
International House. Gravel on the rooftop stone garden requires regular raking.
8
Kiun Kaku. Paths flow sinuously through the main garden.
9 →
The majestic pond and Kikugetsu-tei teahouse at Ritsurin Koen, a major stroll garden in Takamatsu.

The subtle world of associative ideas, symbolism and concealed meanings common to former garden eras was lost in a more generic drive to please the eye. Discourse on garden aesthetics all but vanished. This period is notable for its relatively poor level of scholarship. Gifted garden designers were liberated from the models of the past, but so were the less talented, now free to create substandard work. In this aesthetic and conceptual hiatus, themes, symbolism and abstraction receded, as gardens reverted to being extensions of homes owned by the wealthy and powerful.

The unexamined embrace of Western materialism in the Meiji era resulted in undigested architectural designs, the uncoordinated setting of modern structures alongside traditional buildings and the frequently mismatched pairing of residential and garden styles. In his influential *Art of the Landscape Garden in Japan*, Tamura Tsuyoshi highlighted the clash, noting that these ill-considered, pseudo-foreign homes and gardens were 'wedged, as it were, into spacious Japanese gardens'. The situation improved with the emergence of a new class of garden designers and academics, and the creation of professional bodies like the Japan Garden Association and the Japanese Institute of Landscape Architecture. Much appreciated by Modernist Western architects who were supportive of the idea of spatial continuity, the publication in 1928 of Jiro Harada's *The Japanese Garden* offered images of landscapes viewed from inside buildings, the carefully coordinated framing of gardens emphasizing the relationship between interior and exterior.

Significantly, the pre-war era ended with the creation in 1939 of an iconic garden in the grounds of Tofuku-ji, a Rinzai sect temple in Kyoto. This design represented the revival of symbolism and abstraction in the form of a thoroughly modern landscape, an example of what its creator, a young Shigemori Mirei, would call 'timeless modernity'.

6

7

8

PROJECT
Murin-an
LOCATION
Nanzen-ji Kusakawa-cho, Sakyo-ku, Kyoto
DESIGNER
Ogawa Jihei
YEAR
1896

34

After the old imperial capital was relocated to Tokyo, an event marking the birth of the Meiji era, Kyoto administrators began advocating modernization as a way to forestall the decline of their city. One important manifestation of this new vision was the Lake Biwa Canal, a public engineering work completed in 1890.

The canal played a major part in the garden at Arimoto Yamagata's Murin-an villa, located a little south of Nanzen-ji Temple. Yamagata had been experimenting with flowing water and pioneered the use of drawn water exclusively for irrigating a private garden. A major military and political figure of the Meiji era (1868–1912), with a keen interest in and considerable knowledge of landscape design, he hired Ogawa Jihei (1860–1933), a master gardener, who set about transforming Yamagata's template into one of the first modern gardens of the age.

Ogawa created a V-shaped space between two small woods at the back of the wedge-shaped garden, to frame the distant Higashiyama Hills. Water was diverted from the canal and fed through a small filtering cascade, which flows into a shallow pond, forming a tracery of brooks passing over the gently sloping site. Water crosses the garden diagonally, creating an open space, a foreground that contrasts strikingly with the wooded backdrop. In a clever illusion, the streams seem to flow down from distant hillsides rather than a man-made canal. The aquatic features of the largely horizontal gardens Ogawa created succeed in expanding space and dimension. The east–west axis of the garden is broad in the middle and narrow at each end, a typical Ogawa configuration.

Ogawa's detractors among the Tokyo garden fraternity dubbed his works *sakuteiteki no niwa*, meaning artificial gardens with an overdependence on lineage. Perhaps there was a touch of professional envy in the jibe, given that Ogawa's gardens were considerably less contrived than Edo-period stroll gardens, with their allusive habit of incorporating representations of famous historic and scenic sights in Japan and China, a practice Ogawa eschewed. Early garden writer Loraine Kuck wrote of Ogawa gardens that 'their sole aim is to be as much like nature as possible – nature in its most enchanting and ideal moments'.[1]

In the innovative act of favouring naturalism over symbolism, they signal a significant shift towards the modern Japanese garden.

1
A garden that provides both respite and shade.

1

2

2
Wildfowl are attracted to the shallow waters of the garden.
3
Carefully placed rocks reinforce the stream's embankments.

37

3

4
Gravel pathways wind through the quiet tree cover.
5
A man-made waterfall with natural components.
6
The Eastern Hills form part of the garden's 'borrowed view'.

4

5

PROJECT

LOCATION

YEAR

Kyu Asakura-tei
Sarugaku-cho, Shibuya-ku, Tokyo
1919

40

To call Tokyo a garden city challenges strong preconceptions of the capital as a concrete jungle. Viewed from the perspective of skyscrapers, corporate towers and rooftop observatories, the capital can look like an exercise in thwarting nature, suppressing greenery in the misguided cause of progress. Descend to ground level, however, and a horizontal view of Tokyo reveals one of the highest concentrations of formal gardens of any Asian capital. One such landscape is the Kyu Asakura-tei, or Kyu Asakura Garden.

Asakura Torajiro, the owner of the estate, was an influential Tokyo assembly chairman and rice merchant. Commissioned in 1919, the villa, one of the few remaining traditional wooden residences in the capital, is located in the upscale Daikanyama neighbourhood of western Tokyo. A survivor of two catastrophic events in the city's history, the Great Kanto Earthquake of 1923 and the fire bombings of the Second World War, the home and garden provide an insight into the lives and aesthetic predilections of the Japanese elite at the time.

Condemned, like much of Tokyo's material heritage, to demolition and redevelopment, the villa and garden were spared due to the efforts of architect Maki Fumihiko, who pushed for the preservation of a site exemplifying Taisho-era residential design and landscaping. The villa, made from carefully selected timber, including costly cross-grain cedar, is rendered in the *sukiya-zukuri* style. Utilizing natural materials, particularly wood, *suki* signifies refinement, hinting at the cultivated tastes associated with the tea ceremony.

On the southwestern side of Sarugaku-cho Hill, the paths are positioned at different elevations, adding interest to a garden that, with a dense planting of dwarf bamboo, recreates the inner depths of a deciduous woodland. Closer to the perimeter of the villa, the garden is more formal, its opulent moss and dark, flat stones evoking the ambience of a *cha-niwa*, or tea garden. Listed as an Important Cultural Property, the garden and villa have been open to the public since 2004.

Like other gardens in the capital, the Kyu Asakura-tei can be admired not just for its aesthetic appeal, but for one of the primary functions of Japanese gardens: to expand space and decelerate time.

1
This shallow water bowl adds a modern touch to the garden ornamentation.

1

2

3

4

2
Large foreground stones match the spacious dimensions of the villa.

3
An *engawa* - inner corridor - offers choice views of the garden.

4
Unusually large water basins are a feature of these gardens of the wealthy.

5

6

7

5
Unusually large stone lanterns and stepping stones are a feature of this type of garden.
6
The garden's elegant entrance gate, with a traditional cedar-bark roof.
7
Roof finials sunk into the earth add a touch of refinement to a stroll through the garden.
8
The inner garden combines English naturalism with Japanese stone garden features.

45

8

KYU ASAKURA-TEI

PROJECT

Kiun Kaku

LOCATION

Showa-cho, Atami

YEAR

1919

Kiun Kaku, located in the coastal hot spring of Atami, is a fine example of the designs constructed in the short Taisho era (1912–26), which embraced a slightly modified version of values from the previous Meiji period.

The ownership of decent-sized plots like this in Japan has been, and remains, the prerogative of the affluent, particularly in increasingly urbanized areas like Atami, a popular hot spring resort, where gardens occupy precious real estate. Commissioned by shipping magnate and railroad tycoon Kaichiro Nezu, the garden dates from 1919, with additions made in the 1930s. Creating order from the unmanaged elements of nature had a special appeal to Japan's nouveau riche, who were the architects of change.

By the time Kiun Kaku was conceived, some of the infatuation with Western gardens and design forms had waned, and landscape designers were reasserting their identity by integrating both foreign and indigenous principles into their projects. Ito Teiji, an important garden scholar, endorsed this tendency, writing that it was permissible to see 'distorted versions of foreign ideas existing side by side with primitive, indigenous garden forms'.[1]

Although lawns had been grown in Japanese gardens like Koraku-en in Okayama City, and appeared as grass mounds in landscapes such as the Shuizen-ji Joju-en, an Edo-period garden in Kumamoto, they were used in the grounds of villas like Kiun Kaku to promote the feeling of a parkland. The garden was planted with azaleas, wisteria, Japanese quince, fragrant olive, shrubs and bushes. Many of its miniature foreground trees and taller rear specimens, which create a backdrop and a sense of peripheral density, are evergreens.

Unlike the earlier circuit gardens, there are no *shakkei*, or borrowed views, here. The garden folds in on itself, creating an air of privacy and privilege.

There are some minor lapses of taste, such as the inclusion of a bronze crane statue stooping over the edge of a pond, but discernment wins out in the overall scheme of the garden. The fusion of interior and exterior, a feature of Japanese gardens and structures such as temples and private homes, is skilfully managed.

1
Traditional elements, like pine and azalea trees, feature in this modern garden.

1

KIUN KAKU

2

2
First-floor guest rooms ranged along the garden's small pond.
3
A seamless merging of garden and villa.
4 →
The garden's sloping, well-contoured lines.

3

KIUN KAKU

5

5
The garden design successfully merges different graduated areas.

A Sacred Flower

On first sighting, the white Madonna lily seems a plain enough flower, unlikely to inspire more than prosaic meditations on its beauty, but to devout followers of Christianity in the Middle Ages, it would, by simple association, have been accorded a degree of symbolism that elevated its meaning and inspired faith. Early Christians, exposed to images of the lily in devotional paintings, understood its connection to a legend claiming the Virgin Mary's tomb filled with the flower after her assumption to heaven. The Venerable Bede, an Anglo-Saxon scholar and Benedictine monk, insisted that the petals of the flower represented her unblemished body, its golden stamens her refulgent soul.

Flowers as symbols of the divine flourish in Japan's temple precincts and gardens, principal among them the lotus. A symbol of esoteric Buddhism, it is identified with the deity Kannon, its buds representing salvation for the faithful. In the lotus ponds of Jodo Shinshu, the Pure Land order, the broad, pulpy leaves serve as seats for Amitabha Buddha and attendant divinities. In this manifestation of the Buddha, the deity is depicted at the centre of mandalas, floating on the surface of a garden pond. The dreamscapes depicted in Pure Land Buddhism bear a striking likeness to early models of the Paradise Garden.

Known as the sacred lotus, as well as, variously, the Chinese waterlily, Indian lotus and Egyptian sacred bean, the species commonly found in Japan is *Nelumbo nucifera*. Its association with Buddhism dates from the sixth century, when teachings were brought from continental Asia. In Japanese, the lotus is called *hasu*, a contraction of *hachi-no-su*, meaning bee's nest. Riddled with holes, the plant's seed chamber is said to bear a strong resemblance to the cells of the Japanese paper wasp, the *ashinaga-bachi*.

In the east, the flower grows in the muddy sediment of ponds, a dark and viscous place, which represents the sullied, mortal world. Ascending from defilement, its leaves rise above the water line. As their buds unfold, the flowers become synonymous with spiritual growth, the expectation of enlightenment. It is no coincidence that one of the central postures in Hatha Yoga, is the *padmasana*, the lotus position, adopted by practitioners striving to attain the higher levels of consciousness.

Droplets of water sit in the dry seed chambers of the flower.

PROJECT

LOCATION

DESIGNER

YEAR

International House of Japan Roppongi, Minato-ku, Tokyo Ogawa Jihei 1930

54

With the exception of dry landscape installations, whose lines and components are determined by stone settings that can retain the same sight lines for centuries, Japanese gardens have undergone considerable changes in form and dimension as the result of climatic conditions, urban development, prevailing design trends and, above all, ownership.

In the case of International House, a Modernist building serving as a cultural exchange venue, hotel and events facility, located in a residential section of Roppongi, a fashionable Tokyo district, ownership passed in the Edo period from the Kyogoku clan to the powerful Iwasaki family, founders of the Mitsubishi Company. After a brief spell of government ownership after the Second World War, the plot was taken over by International House. The current building, though extensively renovated in 2005, dates from 1955, making it, by Tokyo standards, almost a heritage structure. It was designed by three leading Japanese architects – Sakakura Junzo, Yoshimura Junzo and Maekawa Kunio – and took around one year to build. Although it was influenced by the Modernist movement in architecture, spearheaded by Le Corbusier, the seamlessly flowing convergent lines between building and garden suggest a more distinctly Japanese aesthetic. Cantilevered over the pond, the restaurant-café section of the building was based on a design taken from Heian-period (794–1185) scroll paintings.

The garden we see today, completed in 1930, was redesigned by the influential gardener Ogawa Jihei (1860–1933). Known for his requisitioning of borrowed views, Ogawa's gardens are characterized by wide, open spaces that integrate lawns and water. Amasaki Hiromasa, a professor at Kyoto University of Art and Design, has written of Ogawa's work, 'His manner of expression was influenced by a modern view of nature and implied departure from the clichéd reproduction of poem scenery. It was in a sense a shift from gardens for contemplation to gardens for appreciation with all five senses.'[1]

The garden strata conform to the classic Japanese approach of dividing landscapes into three portions. In this case, the foreground is dominated by a lawn, the mid-section is planted with bushes and shrubs and the denser background consists of a tree-studded hill.

The pressures on gardens located within areas of prime real estate are nowhere higher than in Tokyo, a city that has shown time and again that redevelopment can trump beauty and heritage. Mercifully, the current custodians of Ogawa's garden and its Modernist addition have made sure it remains dedicated not to commercial advancement, but to lifting the spirits of its visitors.

1
The centre's restaurant is cantilevered over the pond, a traditional garden technique.

1

INTERNATIONAL HOUSE OF JAPAN

2

2
Winding paths add scale and diversity to the garden.
3
A Shinto priest and maiden prepare for rituals connected with a wedding ceremony.

3

4
The garden creates density and mass with the intensive planting of trees and bushes.

4

5
In spring, cherry blossom forms a carpet over some of the garden paths.

6
This bamboo gate adds a traditional touch to a largely modern garden.

7
Gravel on the rooftop stone garden requires regular raking.

5

6

PROJECT

LOCATION

YEAR

Yamamoto-tei
Shibamata, Katsushika-ku, Tokyo
1930

An elegant villa that blends the Zen-influenced *shoin-zukuri* style of the Muromachi era (1336–1573) with European residential architectural features, the building was the residence of Yamamoto Einosuke, the founder of a camera parts manufacturing company. It features the extensive use of natural wood, removable fittings and bright, spacious rooms. The current villa and garden, the subject of extensive renovation, date from 1930.

Originally associated with the living quarters of Zen abbots and chambers serving as temple guest halls, the *shoin-zukuri* residential architectural style was also applied to mansions for high-ranking members of the military. The name *shoin* derives from temple rooms set aside for the study of Buddhist sutras.

Broad windows, set against an *engawa*, or viewing corridor, are designed to frame the garden in the manner of a large painting. As this is a three-dimensional creation, however, viewers can shift perspective and alter depth of view from within the tearooms facing the garden, and from an accessible outside terrace. It is not possible to enter the garden. Designed to be observed from indoors, the pictorial landscape was created to be part of the house, not an ancillary to it.

Although the grounds only cover around 900 square metres (9,688 square feet), the masterly disposition of space creates the illusion of a greater area. Depth is achieved by massing large stepping stones in the foreground, filling the middle ground with a pond, bridges and a waterfall and planting a dense background area of evergreen trees.

Almost inordinately large *yuki-tsuri*, wigwam-shaped bamboo frames supported with poles and ropes, appear at the forefront of the garden, their dimensions in keeping with the gigantism favoured by the owners of gardens during the Taisho era. With climate change, the original function of the frames, to protect trees and shrubs from heavy snow, is less imperative now, the *yuki-tsuri* in the Tokyo region consigned to elegant obsolescence.

The adoption and modification of *shoin*-style architecture and garden principles during the Meiji and Taisho eras was the result of both aesthetic preferences and a desire among the nouveau riche to align themselves with high culture. Unapologetically built to impress, the visual synergy between the villa and garden was also an expression of the social and economic status enjoyed by the Yamamoto family.

1
Stone objects, like lanterns and pagodas, add visual interest.

1

2

3

2
Ripples from the carp-filled pond.

3
Skilfully placed rocks create a pond perimeter.

4

5

4
Straw mats wrapped around tree trunks protect them in the winter.

5
A mellow afternoon light adds atmosphere to the garden.

The Aesthetic Lexicon

On first acquaintance, Japanese garden aesthetics can seem impossibly complex, their terms possessing a range of different meanings. A knowledge of their encoded significance as they are applied in design concepts opens doors into the meaning of the Japanese garden.

Concepts such as *koko* (precious simplicity), *seijaku* (absolute stillness) and *yugen* (unfathomable depth, beauty and subtle profundity), vital to the principles of Japanese garden design, may baffle the uninitiated, but begin to make sense when viewed in the setting of both traditional and modern Japanese gardens.

Eschewing ostentation, *furyu* signifies elegant refinement, *miyabi* refers to refined taste and elegance, a profound subtlety, *kodai* stands for antiquity, *soboku* signifies artless simplicity and *seijaku* stands for tranquillity. *Hen*, meaning mutability, and *fuhen*, permanence, encompass the dual nature of time.

Wabi-sabi is the best known of all the Japanese aesthetics. *Wabi* implies understated qualities such as rustic simplicity, frugality and asymmetrical harmony, the beauty of imperfection. Zen writer and scholar Suzuki Daisetz defined it as 'an active, aesthetic appreciation of poverty'.[1] A garden teahouse, made from wood, reed mats, cedar bark roofs and earthen walls, will try to evoke this mood. *Sabi* stirs a sense of loneliness, a wilderness of sensation, but more specifically denotes the virtues of the worn and neglected, the subtle patination and discolorations of age. A common example might be the maturating effect of moss and lichen on stones, or the unintended beauty of a garden's decomposing clay wall. This is analogous to the catalytic role played by mould and spore in the preparation of certain kinds of Japanese food and in fermentation techniques.

Wabi-sabi, an appreciation of the worn, discarded, beautifully aged, would seem antithetical to the modern garden, until we consider the central Japanese aesthetic of perishability. This is based on the Buddhist concept of *mujo*, usually translated as 'impermanence'. Stability and durability are illusions. Unable to forestall decay, the only solution is to celebrate it, to reevaluate it as an aesthetic.

What all of these aesthetic principles have in common is that they represent a very Japanese preference, still firmly retained in the minds of contemporary landscape designers, for the implicit over the explicit.

A circular *marumado*, moon window, with a winter silhouette of plum branches.

PROJECT
Okochi Sanso

LOCATION
Tabushiyama-cho, Saga Ogurayama, Ukyo-ku, Arashiyama

DESIGNER
Okochi Denjiro

YEAR
1931

Prosperous families, politicians and plutocrats were the main patrons of spacious private gardens in the pre-war era, but in the case of Okochi Sanso, the well-planned landscape was funded by Okochi Denjiro, a popular stage and film star of the day. The common factors in the creation of such gardens were wealth and a desire among the nouveau riche to align themselves with the culture and prestige enjoyed by older families in their role as patrons of the arts.

Okochi was a devout Buddhist, the founder of a Buddha Hall at the foot of Mount Ogura in the verdant Arashiyama district west of Kyoto. The garden he commissioned stands on the southeast side of the gently sloping peak. Construction of the 20,000-square-metre (215,278-square-foot) site took place in the 1930s and took into careful consideration existing landforms, applying compositional laws grounded in the Western naturalism that inspired so many of these gardens.

The mountain resonates with literary allusions, one of the most iconic being that it was where the classic *Ogura Hyakunin'isshu* (Ogura Anthology of One Hundred Poems by One Hundred Poets) was compiled by the twelfth-century bard Fujiwara-no-Teika.

Two obvious legacies from the earlier Meiji and Taisho eras' infatuation with Western naturalism, and their departure from the rigid canons of taste that saw gardens as works of art, are spacious areas of lawn and more diverse vegetation. If these embody a greater freedom of interpretation, contemporary borrowings from the West are counter-balanced by the fact that Okochi Sanso represents, along with similar villa–garden combinations, a return to the Heian-era idea of gardens as integral to residences.

Other examples of historical elements in this twentieth-century garden are the inclusion of a *shakkei* (borrowed view) of Mount Arashi, the Hozukyo Gorge, Mount Hiei, Buddhist statuary, a small Shinto shrine, stepping stones winding through mossy ground cover, a pavilion for moon viewing, a traditional teahouse and an exterior tea gazebo with sweeping views of Kyoto below.

The garden's luxurious foliage and flowers were planted to allow visitors to enjoy the scenery throughout the four seasons. Glancing at the surrounding hills, forests and bamboo groves, there are none of the offending power lines or apartment blocks that have been allowed to occlude many Japanese gardens.

1
Roof tiles have been embedded in the path as repurposed objects.

1

2
The garden's thatched villa is surprisingly modest.
3
Expansive lawns were popular in pre-war gardens like this.

2

3

4
A small Shinto shrine nestled in the depths of the garden.

4

5

6

7

5
Judiciously placed Buddhist statues much older than the garden dot the landscape.
6
Carefully selected rocks create a pleasing composition along a stone path.
7
A thatched gate breaks the monotony of stone steps.
8
The beds of gravel create the impression of a small valley.

75

8

OKOCHI SANSO

PROJECT
LOCATION
DESIGNER
YEAR

Tofuku-ji Temple
Honmachi, Higashiyama-ku, Kyoto
Shigemori Mirei
1939

Completed in 1939, the gardens at Tofuku-ji grew out of an encounter between the head priest of an impoverished temple and a penniless young gardener. Despite being the head temple of the Tofuku-ji sect of Rinza Zen Buddhism, it lacked the funds necessary to pay for a landscape design that would match its prestige.

In exchange for creating and supervising the construction of new gardens encircling the temple *hojo* (main hall), Shigemori Mirei, a relatively untested designer, was offered full board and a free hand to implement his ideas. 'We will not interfere with your work,' head priest Saido Sonoisan assured Shigemori, adding that he was free to 'do whatever you see fit'. In an unusual arrangement, Saido promised Shigemori that, in return for his masterplan, the temple would 'pray for your soul, now and forever'. Shigemori's design would be his first major garden project and, more significantly, an important model for landscape designs in the post-war period.

Shigemori's Hasso-no-niwa (Garden of Eight Views) is actually a quartet of independent segments, beginning with the south garden, where four stone groupings symbolize the Islands of the Immortals. The far corner of this garden consists of five moss-covered mounds, representing Kyoto's five Zen sects. The precisely clipped azaleas in the west garden mirror a geometrical form called *seiden*, which derives from a Chinese method for dividing land. Another design of great originality, the moss garden north of the *hojo* is studded with an irregular grid of flat stones, a chequerboard pattern known as *ichi-matsu*. Suggestive of distant hills, banks of azalea bushes occupy the background, adding mass. The cosmic realm appears in the design of the east garden, the Garden of the Big Dipper, where the recycled base columns of the temple urinals are placed in cloud-shaped white sand, in a form intended to replicate the configuration of Ursa Major, the Great Bear or Plough constellation.

Each of these cardinally orientated designs, refreshing in their reinterpretation of tradition, aptly expresses Shigemori's mission to create gardens for the modern age.

1
Clipped hedges form a pattern known as *seiden*.

1

TOFUKU-JI TEMPLE

2

3

2
Powerful rock clusters like this typify Shigemori Mirei's work.

3
Five moss-covered mounds represent Kyoto's five Zen sects.

4
The northern garden's celebrated moss design, known as *ichimatsu*.

4

TOFUKU-JI TEMPLE

Tim Richardson

80 Tradition and Innovation in Planting in Modern Japanese Gardens

1

2

The span of this book covers a number of phases of landscape-design development over the course of around 140 years, beginning in the decades that followed Japan's 'opening up' to the world after the so-called Meiji Restoration of 1868. This was a period of rapid cultural change that affected most aspects of Japanese culture, with garden and landscape design being no exception. The result was that after a long period of consistency and stability in terms of garden style and horticultural practice, the twentieth century saw a number of new phases of development occurring in relatively quick succession.

One constant, however, has been the native Japanese flora, which has remained the focus of the horticultural aspect of the country's gardens even as new plants – notably brightly coloured perennial flowers familiar from the European herbaceous tradition – became more prevalent. Notwithstanding this influx of new plants and 'foreign' styles of garden, such as rose gardens, the underlying Japanese attitude to plants and planting has remained the same, with certain native trees and flowers still privileged above others. The almost reverential attitude towards subjects such as pines, maples, lotus and flowering cherries – to name a few – has not been extended to the 'imported' botanical vocabulary of the twentieth century. This means that even the most 'modern' Japanese garden will frequently contain traditional plants, or groupings of them, which are freighted with complex and nuanced symbolic and cultural meanings that have accreted over many centuries. Cherry blossom, for example, is related to the concept of human mortality and the fleetingness of life, while the pine tree signifies endurance, constancy and strength of character. It is simply not possible for such plants to be used in gardens in Japan without associative inferences being communicated and understood.

As Ito Teiji put it in *Japanese Garden: An Approach to Nature* (1972):

> 'In the Oriental garden it is nature and not the gardener which does the creating. The line of a stone, the mass of a tree, the contour of a hillock – all of these things are observed and worked into a pattern which the garden architect has perceived, a pattern which, because it is natural, is unique. Since he is always inside his garden, the viewer is surprised by a new vista, an unexpected view – he arranges for it. His natural garden will change with the seasons, just as those who see the garden will change with the years.'

Furthermore, the attempt to apprehend the essence of things, which is at the heart of the Buddhist attitude to gardens, means that in some ways the concept of seasonality is rendered unimportant. This attitude to gardens is deeply ingrained in Japanese culture. Despite climatic differences across Japan, a symbolic attitude to planting persists in every geographical region of Japan. As Ito explains:

> 'The Japanese garden is like a still picture – a frozen moment which is also all eternity. It remains the same no matter the season because the seasons are acknowledged, and this acknowledgment is spiritual, a combination of idea and emotion.'

All garden cultures around the world are intimately connected with the passage of the seasons, but perhaps it should not be surprising that in the case of Japan, this relationship has been played out in a stylized and at times ritualistic manner. Not just in terms of the symbolism of individual plants, but in relation to geomantic beliefs regarding channels of cosmic energy and how this ultimately has an impact on the health and well-being of a household. A celebration of seasonality is also uniquely played out in other aspects of Japanese cultural life – for example in kimono design, local festivals celebrating specific plants in season, painted decoration of partition doors inside houses and the production of mochi balls or sweets in the shape of maple leaves. Tea ceremony is a seasonally nuanced practice, not least in the way that the smaller and more intimate garden spaces associated with the teahouse, and the journey towards it, allow for intensive examination of plant life as it goes through seasonal change, resulting in a heightened perception and appreciation of nature. There is a famous story concerning Sen no Rikyu (1522–1591), the tea-garden master, which describes an occasion when he had finished raking the leaves off the gravel in his garden. He deliberately shook an overhanging bough so that several fresh leaves fell to the ground, leaving them in place as a reminder of the desirability of imperfection and the imperturbability of nature.

1
The glossy *Monstera deliciosa*, or split-leaf philodendron, can be found in warmer, southern-climate gardens in Japan.

2
A rooftop oculus gives a modern twist on a traditional theme at this inner courtyard landscape at the Kahitsukan, the Kyoto Museum of Contemporary Art.

3

4

The basic plant vocabulary of the Japanese garden is considered to have been established during the Heian period (794–1185), when classic garden texts the *Pillow Book* (995) of Sei Shonagon, the *Sakutei-ki* – or 'record of garden-making' (chiefly concerned with rock placement and water) – and *The Tale of Genji* (both eleventh century) by Murasaki Shikibu were produced. The four gardens described in *The Tale of Genji*, each one related to a specific season and aligned on a cardinal point, are elegant, colourful retreats where visitors can float across still, reflective lakes by boat, composing poetry while enjoying the colours and scents of flowering shrubs and small trees such as deutzia, kerria, azalea, prunus and osmanthus. The tradition of *o-karikomi* or the close-clipping of certain shrubs – notably camellia and azalea bushes – is very ancient but became particularly associated with the master Enshu Kobori (1579–1647); it has remained integral to Japanese garden style ever since, notably in the twentieth-century work of Shigemori Mirei. Bonsai has always been a specialist practice and remains so. These traditional associations and techniques have not been lost in the modern era, but are sometimes hidden or taken for granted.

So Japanese tradition has played into the development of the country's gardens across the twentieth century. In most cases, however, these practices and features will have been diluted somewhat, often to the disappointment of traditionalists. Nevertheless, certain dynamic aspects related to planting remain integral to the experience of Japanese gardens of all periods. Trees very often act as semi-permeable boundaries between the domestic space of the garden and the landscape beyond, especially in the case of bare-trunked pines, which appear to 'mediate' between the garden and the natural world. Trees and shrubs are used as framing devices and as a complement to architecture. Textural aspects such as the contrast between the softer, more amorphous forms of clipped shrubs and the hard, jagged edges of rocks also play a prominent role, as does the use of moss, in its many and various forms, as ground cover. The movement of plants in the wind is sometimes overlooked as a source of pleasure in these 'formal' gardens, as is the presence of birds and insects, flitting in and out of the scene.

Recent decades have seen a new trend emerging in Japanese garden design, in line with the 'naturalistic turn' in garden design that has been gathering pace since the mid-1990s as a reaction to climate change and a perception that what is human-made has been harmful to the environment. This naturalistic style typically deploys larger perennial plants and grasses in swathes, playing on their forms more than their colours and exploiting the aesthetic interest of seedheads and dying stems in late autumn and winter. There are a few recent examples of this style in Japan achieved by European designers. Tokachi Millennium Forest on Hokkaido features a large naturalistic meadow plantation by British designer Dan Pearson, while Dutch plantsman Piet Oudolf has created one of his pictorial meadow gardens at the Hana Biyori natural park in western Tokyo.

Perhaps more in line with Japanese traditions is the trend, over the past decade or so, for naturalistic woodland gardens realized in a style known as *zoki-no-niwa*. These are intensified versions of forest environments found in the wild, deploying native trees such as junipers, maples, camellias, magnolias and yews – 'mixed trees' which create the illusion of natural woodland. A ground cover of mondo grass or moss creates a sense of unity and the feeling of being immersed in a green capsule; a good example is the Abema Tower garden (see page 7). These spaces are reminiscent of the 'woodland quotation' gardens that can often be seen in South Korea – for example prefacing modern office blocks in Seoul, or else in more traditional form as 'sacred groves' at the edges of villages and towns. These designed woodlands in Japan and South Korea are rich in animistic resonances. Perhaps it is not too fanciful to speculate that a feeling of communication with nature tangibly still exists in modern Eastern societies that are perhaps now better known for their high-tech industries and economic aspirations than for their enduring connections with past traditions and the natural environment.

5

3
Drifts that respond to the mountain landscape in Tokachi Millennium Forest's Meadow Garden, Hokkaido by Dan Pearson.

4
The naturalistic Piet Oudolf Garden at the Hama Biyori natural park in Tokyo.

5
At Shugaku-in Imperial Villa (1629), the Upper Garden sits within the forest. It's a key historical example of Shakkei – a 'borrowed view' of landscape beyond the garden confines.

PROJECT

LOCATION

YEAR

Nezu Museum
Minami-Aoyama, Minato-ku, Tokyo
1941

Commissioned by business mogul and prodigious art collector Nezu Kaichiro, this iconic Tokyo garden was completed in 1941. In the pre-war era of economic growth, wealthy patrons gained a taste for acquiring art objects and many of these items are displayed in the museum garden itself.

A superb example of the *shinzan-no-tei*, or *shinzan-yukoku* gardens, which seek to recreate the atmosphere of deep mountains and valleys, the landscape is more evocative of a wild, forested region of Japan than a carefully planned landscape plot in the middle of Tokyo. The garden represents the peak of a taste among the wealthy and discerning for Modernist English and Western naturalism infused with age-old Japanese aesthetics.

Entrance to the grounds is via a long, covered passage planted on one side with bamboo that runs alongside a strip of black *nachiguro* pebbles. The current architectural version of this fine art museum, designed by Kengo Kuma, contains a valuable collection of sculptures, tea ceremony utensils, bronze and lacquer works and calligraphy. Kuma's spacious plate glass windows invite natural light into the first-floor gallery, an effect that backlights Buddhist figures against the garden.

Winding stone paths descend deeper into the multi-layered garden, circumnavigating a sunken pond and a number of rustic teahouses. In the manner of the Edo-era stroll garden, the paths, boring deeper into lush, primal greenery, are arranged to skilfully obscure and then reveal perspectives. The aesthetics of Japanese gardens, the spirit of *wabi sabi*, in which imperfection and natural ageing are encouraged, and the aspirations of religious art converge in a garden that feels like hallowed ground, a dense, spiritually infused sanctuary ingeniously disassociated from the city. There is also an air of profound antiquity, emanating from the placement of beautifully carved and incised Buddhist statuary, ancient road markers, stone lanterns and pagodas, throughout a garden that doubles as an open-air gallery. Here, we encounter a sandstone Standing Buddha Triad dating from China's sixth-century Northern Wei Dynasty, a Seated Bodhisattva, precisely dated 1466, and a Muromachi-era Japanese Ksitigarbha carved panel.

Every April, nature imitates art, when the museum displays a gold-ground painting by the eighteenth-century artist Korin Ogata, a six-panel work depicting a field of irises, a national treasure known as *Irises* (*Kakitsubata*). At the same time as the limited showing, beds of irises in the garden pond come into bloom, their form faithfully replicating Korin's masterwork.

1
The modern covered entrance to the garden and museum.

1

NEZU MUSEUM

2

3

2
A rustic teahouse submerged in greenery.

3
This stylish, modern teahouse is designed to let generous amounts of light in.

4
Backlit autumn foliage adds charm to the garden.

5

6

5
Winding paths reveal fresh perspectives at every turn.
6
An ancient bronze Chinese statue complements the museum's collection of Asian art and sculpture.
7
Stones glisten and acquire extra lustre in the rain.

7

8

8
Seemingly wild, the garden is actually meticulously well maintained.

Cherry Blossoms

The cherry, more than any other flower, has come to symbolize an exquisite but melancholic awareness of the impermanence of life. There is a special poignancy to it that is a blend of wistfulness and longing, a sensation deriving from a very Japanese aesthetic that cherishes the temporary nature of beauty. At its most refined, this corresponds to the ancient aesthetic of *mono no aware*, a difficult concept that might be compared to the Roman poet Virgil's *lacrimae rerum*, 'tears of things'.

The close identification between the Japanese sensibility and the transient beauty of the cherry blossom, the national flower, is acute. One famously smitten writer claimed, 'If someone wishes to know the essence of the Japanese spirit, it is the fragrant cherry blossom in the early morning.'[1]

Few nations have extracted so much pleasure and sadness from the contemplation of a single flower. The splendid but short-lived span of the cherry has inspired countless poems on loss and celebration. Matsuo Basho (1644–1694) had much to say about the blossom, celebrating its timelessness when he wrote the following haiku about a Japanese garden:

Moss-grown,
By the cherry-flowers
A stone water-stand.

The Buddhist nun Chiyo-ni (1703–1775) captured the arresting beauty of the flower in another haiku:

Evening temple bell
Halted in the sky
By cherry blossoms

It is almost impossible to list the number of cherry varietals in Japan. With two to six pink flowers per corymb, the dazzling *somei-yoshino* (Yoshino cherry) is the most common tree in Japan, prompting some critics to say it is overplanted to the exclusion of equally fine cultivars. The *shidare-yoshino* is a weeping varietal, appreciated as much for its graceful form as its blossoms. Cultivated since the Heian period, the delicate *sato-zakura* (Oriental cherry) flowers in clusters, while the white and pale pink *yama-zakura* (mountain cherry) is admired for its tenacity, growing in the poor soil of craggy slopes.

The progress of the flower is a national event, enthusiastically followed in daily reports. From the moment the first *sakura* (cherry blossoms) appear in the southern islands of Okinawa and Kyushu in early March, to the last petals blown from the trees in northern Hokkaido, a day does not pass without the media monitoring the progress of the *sakura zensen*, or 'cherry blossom front'. Teams dutifully report that the flower is *sanbu zaki* (thirty percent open), or *gobu zaki* (fifty percent), before triumphantly announcing that it has reached what is regarded as its most exquisite point: *shichibu zaki* (seventy percent). This is the season for *hanami* (cherry viewing parties). There is some urgency in organizing these events. Though the period for parties lasts up to one week, purists insist that the blossom is at its best for no longer than three days.

Connoisseurs, eschewing crowded *hanami* gatherings, seek out rarer species of trees for quieter aesthetic satisfaction. The perfect moment, they will tell you, is when a slight breeze releases a flurry of blossom into the air, a *hana-fubuki* (petal storm) that dusts the ground with pink and white flowers that are as pure and delicate as snow.

The *somei-yoshino* is the most common cherry tree varietal in Japan, but was only introduced in the nineteenth century.

1

Part 2

The Modern Mindscape: Design since 1945

2

1 ←
The rooftop carbon garden at the Ichihara Lakeside Museum.
2
The sinuous dry river at the National Institute for Materials Science in Tsukuba City.

In the 2021 James Bond film *No Time to Die*, Blofeld, 007's tireless nemesis, is seen sauntering through a neo-Japanese garden built inside a biochemical plant on a disputed island somewhere between Japan and Russia. In this dystopian landscape, junipers, pruned into models of Japanese topiary, are made from Velcro, rocks from silicone. Fabulations like this are nowhere near as implausible as they sound. In the contemporary Japanese garden, you may come across materials as synthetic as carbon fibre, translucent polycarbonate and treated concrete. There are garden rocks made from shimmering fibreglass and hardened plastic.

It is not possible to talk about the contemporary Japanese garden, its innovations and material essence, how it got to this extraordinary stage in its evolution, without invoking the name Shigemori Mirei. By the standards of the day, his designs, which included the early use of unorthodox materials like tiles and coloured pebbles, were uncompromisingly radical. Shigemori's singularly muscular stone arrangements add a fresh, soaring quality, a virility to his gardens. Reacting to what he considered the stale formalism and endless duplication of garden forms, the art's degeneration into mannerism and over-ornamentation, Shigemori believed that, in common with other art forms, gardens needed to evolve.

Garden writer Christian Tschumi described Shigemori's avant-garde designs as a 'compelling manifesto for continuous cultural renewal'.[1] Depending on whether you consult his devotees or detractors, Shigemori's landscapes are either iconoclastic masterpieces or affronts to tradition. Between the years 1924 and 1975, he designed over 180 gardens in Japan, an extraordinary creative output by any standard. Although he was best known as a landscape designer, a master of stone placement, his accomplishments also extended to being a garden scholar, painter, practitioner of the tea ceremony and master of ikebana, or flower-arranging. Alongside these interests, his fascination with contemporary Western art inspired some of his more daring innovations.

Where the great Japanese painter and landscape designer Sesshu Toyo (1420–1506) favoured flat rocks, Shigemori's gardens are notable for their generous (some critics have said excessive) use of vertically set stones, some of which are slightly tilted. A preference for sharp, upright mountain rocks over the smoother surfaces of river stones resulted in audacious stone clusters. Shigemori's skilfully deployed arrangements, with at least half of the rocks placed in the earth for stability, defy conventional wisdom and the strong admonitions found in garden manuals from the Heian and Edo periods, with their portentous warnings against creating clusters of upright rocks in close proximity.

Thoroughly immersed in the masterpieces of a former age, the artist saw himself as a successor to a Modernist spirit emanating from the past. As his grandson Shigemori Mitsuaki expressed it, 'The eternally modern creations of the past, in effect, gave birth to the newest of the modern creators: Mirei.'[2] Shigemori's gardens embody the notion that the most accomplished Japanese landscape designs are not imitations of the natural world, but co-existing forms that harmonize art and nature. He wrote, 'A garden should have a timeless modernity. What is singularly modern in our time has no real value.'[3] His drive to reenergize Japanese landscape design resulted in daring innovations. Like all radical shifts, even ones that pay homage to tradition, his avant-garde designs were divisive. Ultimately, an appreciation of Shigemori's work is a matter of taste, but the gardens are always alert, refreshing and compellingly original.

If Shigemori's interest in and requisitioning of other cultural practices in his gardens reflected the work of older designers who were also tea masters, calligraphers and painters, we see for the first time in Tange Kenzo's 1958 design for the Kagawa Prefectural Office the fusion of landscape designer and modern architect. Creating accessible space, a sharing as opposed to coveting of space, the garden played a key part in moving from the private to the public domain. In Tange's conception, fluid forms were combined with geometrical lines, a spatial infrastructure that had more in common with the modern city than natural landscapes. Stark, dramatic contrasts were achieved by placing rocks, imposing primordial forms, against the reflective planes of glassed-in buildings. With natural sculptural forms complementing the rationalism of modern architecture, the contrast between the garden and buildings creates a powerful monumentality.

Early juxtapositions like this prompted the question of whether it made sense to construct Japanese gardens at the foot of reinforced steel office towers in the centre of crowded metropolises. The conspicuously modern landscapes that appeared in the post-war period could hardly have been more different from their antecedents. At least at first glance. But the changes in design and landscape elements that emerged during this early post-war era were accompanied by a lingering nostalgia for the garden principles of a former age, an affectionate reverence for garden prototypes and traditions, a reluctance to entirely abandon their teachings and inherent wisdom.

The revival in the Showa period (1926–89) of the *karesansui*, or dry landscape garden, facilitated in large part by Shigemori, restored symbolism and abstraction. The construction of Ryogin-an, a sub-temple of Kyoto's Tofuku-ji complex, is instructive. The garden's principal theme is *satori*, or enlightenment. Shigemori's 1960 stone garden is flanked by containing walls, one of which is covered in a long bamboo screen. The vertical design is dramatized with a zig-zag pattern of bamboo rods representing lightning bolts, a symbol for the way that enlightenment strikes. At another Tofuku-ji sub-temple, Komyo-in, Shigemori created a stone arrangement on a mound at the rear of the garden, overlooking clusters of rocks in the mid and foreground zones. The word *komyo* refers to light emerging from the Buddha, which in turn symbolizes wisdom and compassion. In Shigemori's Hashin-tei (Garden of the Moonlight on Waves) design, three rock compositions, known as *sanzon-seki*, represent Gautama Buddha, flanked by Amida Buddha and Yakushi-Nyorai, the Buddha of Healing. These are geometrically linked to stones placed throughout the garden, each representing rays of light emanating from the three deities. In a powerful work of symbolism, we see the Buddha delivering a sermon to a congregation represented by the group of garden stones.

Modern gardens, like art movements, didn't spring into life overnight. Japanese garden design evolved in parallel with an awareness of well-established landscape principles. The stone garden was discovered to have a close stylistic affinity with modern architecture, while rock gardens attached to Zen temples gradually assimilated elements that would turn them into incarnations of a Buddhist worldview. The powerful ambiguities of dry landscape arrangements, the inevitable questions they raise in relation to what constitutes a garden, the profundity of concepts and principles, many of them deriving from Taoism and Zen, never fail to baffle the uninitiated. Many writers, lured by the putative mystique of the gardens, have, after finding themselves out of their depth, reverted to comfortable over-simplifications. When exactly did we start calling these landscapes 'Zen gardens'? The writings of Buddhist scholar Suzuki Daisetz (1870–1966), the garden designer and theorist Takuma Tono (1891–1985) and the Hawaiian-born garden writer Loraine Kuck (1894–1977) helped enforce the connections between Zen and garden principles, linking them with the renaissance of the stone garden. Although the Japanese term *Zen-tei* (Zen garden) exists, it was seldom referred to among non-specialists. Kuck was the first person to use the now generically employed term 'Zen garden' in English.

Unless one insists on perfectly raked gravel, the stone garden is relatively easy to maintain. This partially explains its increasing prominence in modern urban settings, where it creates the comforting illusion of permanence. It was not until the post-war period that hewn rocks, formed into sculptural compositions, began to appear. The chiselled, sometimes hollowed-out rocks we see in many contemporary designs are not about replicating the exact details of landscape. Abstract and sculptural in form, they represent nature transmuted into art. From their origins as spiritual or aesthetic environments, such gardens have acquired the significance of art installations, their crisp verticals and horizontals, compositional frame and firmly controlled field of vision inviting parallels with modern photographic composition and architecture.

Over time, Japanese stone gardens have fared a great deal better than designs that depend on more perishable elements like trees, shrubs and flowers. It's interesting to ponder the irony that, in comparison with the great gardens of England and France, whose horticultural components have been subject to climate change and decay, an overwhelming number of Japanese dry landscape gardens, reflecting a philosophy keenly aware of impermanence, have survived intact.

While today's designers still include many professional *niwashi* and *uekiya*, landscape gardeners focused primarily on maintaining gardens and cultivating trees, they also include town planners, interior designers, sculptors, landscape designers and architects. Among the latter are a less easily defined group of new professionals, people in possession of draughtsmanship skills, but with no formal training in garden construction, who, nevertheless, find themselves attached to public and commercial projects, often working alongside local governments and general contractors.

3

4

5

In a post-war era characterized by economic growth, industrialization and expanding urban zones, gardens have been created for public plazas, the courtyards of government offices, Western-style hotels, concert halls, museums, art galleries, department store rooftops, corporate spaces and even service station shopping zones. Private gardens were once highly valued as status symbols. These days, it is more common to find large residential plots of land sold to developers, who then construct apartment blocks, shopping complexes or tiny private homes with enough frontage for a car, but no garden. Landscapes found in public spots like restaurants, cafés, hot springs and within the atriums of corporate buildings have, therefore, come to act as surrogates for private gardens.

Rather than bowing to the desires of nature, contemporary designers seek to craft a personal vision free of the site-specific or geomantic imperatives of traditional gardens. The modern age has, accordingly, witnessed a shift from the spiritual to the cerebral, with designers projecting their own intellects, aesthetic preferences and layouts onto natural landforms and stone arrangements. Reflecting the post-war adoption of the Western-inspired dualism of man and nature, contemporary Japanese gardens moved from being conceived as *land*-scapes to what might be called *mind*-scapes. Rather than seeking to mirror nature, such gardens increasingly function as mediums for self-expression.

Inspired by the works of multi-disciplinary innovators Shigemori Mirei and Tange Kenzo, new designers flourished in this more liberal milieu. Early examples of experimental design include sculptor Nagare Masayuki's 1961 waterfall for the Palace Hotel in Tokyo, formed from carved rectangles. Set behind glass and reinforced concrete walls like a prized art exhibit, the Longchamp Textile Company's 'Cool Garden', an early 1970s design from Hiroshi Murai, featured a marble courtyard and dried trees covered in silver paint. The naturalistic waterfall visible from the lobby of the ANA Hotel in Kyoto, renamed the ANA Crowne Plaza Kyoto, was, deceptively, made of moulded plastic.

Being up to date in an age self-consciously declaring itself to be modern meant designers could avail themselves of unconventional materials and sites. Garden specialist Oguni Syuichi's assertion that 'one does not create a new garden from completely new materials'[4] no longer held true. Dressed stones, split granite, geometrically patterned stepping stones and lighter, synthetic materials were introduced. Revealing rows of wedging grooves and split edges in rocks became a way of demonstrating a different form of beauty. At its most radical, the geometry of the modern garden completely excludes natural elements like trees and plants, its only concession to nature the occasional inclusion of biomorphic rock forms. In some instances, nature itself has been rejected in favour of manufactured or synthetic substitutes. Architect Hasegawa Itsuko's 1990 design for the Shonandai Cultural Center dispenses entirely with natural materials, its only natural component being water.

Like the predetermined viewing points for stone or moss gardens, arrangements where entrance into the garden proper is forbidden, many designs found in corporate or institutional buildings restrict access by placing gardens in recessed spaces or behind glass.

The architecture emerging in the 1920s, pioneered by European designers like Le Corbusier and Mies van der Rohe, involved reducing construction volumes to flat planes, eliminating ornamentation and embracing asymmetry, ideas in natural accord with Japanese garden design. The metamorphosis of the Japanese garden was influenced by cross-encounters with other cultures. Contemporary landscape artists are free to appropriate whatever influences pass across their field of vision, whether it be the vegetal walls of Patrick Blanc, the terraced earthworks and landforms of Charles Jencks or designs inspired by the ancient astronomical gardens of India.

3
Soaring rocks, like these at the Kishiwada Castle Garden, are a characteristic of Shigemori Mirei's work.

4
A granite bench in the grounds of the Kagawa Prefectural Government Office encourages passersby to stop, sit and reflect.

5
According to its designer, the contemporary garden at Zuiganzan Enkou-ji Temple was inspired by the spirit of Buddhism.

6

6
The Teshima House Garden, a transgressive Pop Art design.
7
A synthetic version of traditional winding streams at the Shonandai Cultural Center.
8 →
Shigemori Mirei's trademark coloured gravel at Fukuchi-in Temple.

It is no coincidence that many recent garden designs are paired with daring new structural forms. Such gardens represent a shift from a formal adherence to rules of perspective dictated by the art of painting to the ever-evolving principles of urban landscaping and architecture. Like architecture and sculpture, gardens are inherently spatial, temporal, four-dimensional. Of all the innovative movements in the visual arts, Cubism comes closest, in its interacting geometric forms and angularity, to modern garden design. Nature, it is understood, is incapable of producing a perfectly straight line. As Benoit Mandelbrot wrote in *The Fractal Geometry of Nature*: 'Clouds are not spheres, mountains are not cones, coastlines are not circles, and bark is not smooth, nor does lightning travel in a straight line.' In dealing with the challenges of building gardens in crowded cities, of juxtaposing natural forms with the geometry of the urban grid, Japanese designers can draw from an abundance of tried and tested design models, ranging from the compressed gardens of medieval temples and private residences to the confining parameters of the tea garden and the inventiveness required in creating the tiny *tsubo-niwa* courtyard gardens for space-inhibited, urban merchant homes.

In the context of Japan's perpetually mutating cities, landscape designers are rethinking ways in which gardens can exist in contemporary urban settings. Although master garden designer Yasumoro Sadao has written, 'Don't look only at gardens: look at the entire landscape',[5] this advice is frequently overlooked by construction companies unconcerned about adding to the clutter of Japanese cities. The traditional perspective-altering technique of *shakkei*, creating a visual continuum from foreground to distant background, is still practised, but in the urban context, with a bricolage of intrusive buildings distracting attention from the garden, exclusion is often more important than incorporation. In the ever-changing environment of Japanese cities, the modern garden offers the prospect of spatial stability, creating repositories of future memory in metropolises where there is little hesitation about eviscerating heritage.

7

The modern mindscape rarely exists entirely independently from the past. The contemporary designer mediates allusions to the Japanese garden, while insisting on a personal vision potentially at odds with tradition, but often incorporating, consciously or otherwise, aspects of it. One of the foremost landscape designers practising today, Masuno Shunmyo, is both a curator of tradition and an astonishing innovator. His aim as a practising Soto Zen priest, landscape artist and mindful living authority is to create gardens as a respite from the pressures of daily life. 'The garden,' he has written, 'is a special spiritual place where the mind dwells.'[6] Favouring rock, the most primal material of all, Masuno designs gardens that are expressive of a keen intelligence and profound knowledge of Japanese culture, combined with an artist's perspective on landscape. The work draws the viewer into the production process itself. Visible on many of his rocks are cracks and drill marks, indicating quarry work, a statement on the combined power of nature and creative human intervention.

In accord with the eleventh-century garden manual *Sakutei-ki*, which inveighs garden makers with the instruction, *ishi no kowan wo shitagahite*, 'follow the request of rocks', Masuno dedicates time to 'listen' to stones before setting them. Engaging in dialogue with a garden may sound like the act of a shaman rather than a landscape designer, but it is integral to the traditional idea of telepathic collaboration, of establishing contact with a garden plot and its *jigokoro*, or 'spirit of place'. This elevated level of communication sees the designer in the role of a medium, an amanuensis.

Applying a powerfully Zen-infused approach to design, Masuno, who has worked on temples, hotels, private company and residential gardens, a university campus, research centre and library, believes gardens are close to fine art. When asked for his view on the use of materials such as concrete and carbon fibre, Masuno supported change, with the caveat that 'the first thing to consider when creating a modern Japanese garden is whether the material will retain its presence for hundreds of years'. He added, 'Ageing is not the same as deterioration.'[7]

9

10

One of the ironies of contemporary city gardens is that the Japanese preference for minimalism confronts a propensity to indulge in maximum visibility. This is partly achieved by lighting. Illumination in the urban garden is quite different from the natural effects evident in traditional gardens. The physiognomy of stone altered by the reflections from glass plate, polished marble and granite walls, the mirage-like impact and atmospheric transformations caused by strong sunlight on concrete, infuses materials with the luminescence of modern architectural surfaces.
In striking contrast to their ancestors, contemporary Japanese adore light, their great cities brilliantly illuminated. By the time the novelist Junichiro Tanizaki had published his 1933 essay on Japanese aesthetics 'In Praise of Shadows', an older appreciation of muted light had already begun to lapse into a cult of quaintness. The author celebrates the merits of meagre light and perishable, organic materials, noting in the case of the *zashiki*, the Japanese tatami room, that walls are deliberately made from soil and sand, in order to 'let the frail, melancholic, ephemeral light saturate the solemn composure of their earthy tones'. Tanizaki pays keen attention to the shadows that lurk in lintels, beneath temple eaves and in alcoves, sensitive to minute details like the sombre, trance-like beauty of gold leaf-covered doors and screens, catching morsels of light entering a room from the garden.

If there is a contemporary tendency to try and improve or subvert nature, this also applies to the use of shadow and light. Is it really necessary, we wonder, to illuminate cherry blossoms and bracts of wisteria with cumbersome, intrusive lamps? Although some gardens use portable luminaires in the manner of old *roji andon*, the washi paper lamps once used to subtly illuminate the stepping stones of tea gardens, artificial lighting all too often means unsightly lamp fixtures and electric cords close to gravel borders and rocks. In the past, the moon, oil lamps and candles placed in the chambers of stone lanterns were enough. For largely commercial reasons rather than aesthetic ones, many gardens today are equipped with clusters of LED lamps and bulbs, which replicate daylight rather than the natural, infinitely more nuanced illumination of nocturnal gardens lit by a shifting interplay of moon and cloud. The misconception here is that brilliant lighting reveals gardens in their entirety, when in fact, its effect is to eviscerate their essence.

Despite Masuno's conviction that tradition and modernity can co-exist, there is less concern in the contemporary garden about adhering to older imperatives like geomancy, taking measures to ward off malign spirits or transgressing ancient taboos. According to ancient gardening rules linked to natural phenomena, misfortune might come to the owner of a garden if a stone that was found standing at a vertical angle was placed horizontally, the latter position suggesting collapse or death. In another example, visitations by evil forces could be averted by planting a cycad (*sotetsu*), a plant with sharp, repelling ferns, at the entrance to a garden. It is doubtful today's landscape designers, liberated from the past, are quite so inhibited about tampering with the natural order, especially those striving to align gardens with art.
As a result, gardens have, to some extent, been demystified. We are no longer required to decipher their meanings or inner enigmas, because designers have conveniently provided us with detailed explanations and technical notes. It is standard practice now to create precisely formulated plans before proceeding to construct a garden, adopting a Western approach to architecture that did not exist in Japan until the post-war era. A more intuitive approach to design was common in the past, although ink brush sketches were occasionally used to determine scale. In most cases, however, layouts evolved during construction, accommodating ongoing adjustments and timely moments of inspiration.

11

9
A very Modernist open garden recess at the Kyoto International Conference Center.

10
A dynamic arrangement of rocks, representing the Canadian Shield, in the Canadian Embassy dry landscape garden.

11
The landscaped grounds of the Kyoto International Conference Center.

12

12
An ocean and horizon view from an inner corridor of the Enoura Observatory.

13
The Umeda Sky Building soaring above Ando Tadao's Wall of Hope.

14 →
A sea of billowing waves or green islets at Rinsho-ji, a temple garden deep in the Osaka countryside.

The question of whether gardens are an art form is very much part of the modern discussion, but it likely never occurred to eighteenth-century European collectors and literati. It was assumed that gardens took their assigned place alongside painting, sculpture, recitals and more mystical forms of religious devotion. That colossus of Regency-era English garden design, Humphry Repton, declared, 'Gardens are works of art rather than of nature.'[8] The Japanese would doubtless define their finest gardens as works of art, but with the proviso that they are always framed with a symbolic vision of nature in mind. In Japanese gardens, landscapes are not imitations of the natural world, but forms that harmonize art and nature. The Japanese landscape gardener, an artist in nature, goes a step further, holding up a mirror to aspects of human nature. Constructing a Japanese garden provides the opportunity to create a form that might be called organic art, by reinterpreting aspects of encountered nature. A diversity of forms, ranging from scenes created according to the strict directives of ancient garden manuals to modern, iconoclastic designs, is reflected in the Japanese garden and its search for a place in the world of applied and fine art.

A feature of iconic works of art is their tendency to break with precedents. Designing within the parameters of tradition, emblematic landscapes, like the aristocratic Vaux-le-Vicomte, the temple installation of Ryoan-ji and the circuit garden of Katsura Rikyu, are examples of older leaps in innovation associated with art. When we talk about the art of gardening, the emphasis is not on gardens as venerated art objects, but on the process of designing and making a landscape, which requires an order of skill that *is* artistic.

It may not be possible in the contemporary context to experience the same unearthly calm afforded by an old temple or tea garden, but even with today's landscape designs, more dependent on sculptured rocks and synthetic materials for their effects, the principles deeply embedded within modern gardens may still connect us to the greater natural world. The tireless experimentation involved in making the new Japanese garden offers a different, no less valuable quality of experience. In unsettling us, trip-wiring expectations and assumptions, its most original designs, whether understood as reinterpretations of prototypical landscapes, art installations or mind sanctuaries, succeed with consummate flair.

1
3

PROJECT

Shigemori Mirei Garden Museum

LOCATION

Yoshida Sakyoku, Kyoto

DESIGNER

Shigemori Mirei

YEAR

1943

108

One of the most original garden designers in the history of the art, Shigemori Mirei (1896–1975) drew both admirers and detractors. Even today, his critics face off against fierce defenders of his ideas. At the Shigemori Mirei Garden Museum in Kyoto, we find a garden containing many of his signature design preferences.

The fact that Shigemori's home looks out onto one of his own creations is a convincing self-endorsement. Here we find a large rock, shaped like a vessel and placed in gravel raked into wave shapes. The rock is from Awa in Shikoku, a region well known for its blue chlorite schist, a common stone in Shigemori gardens.

The house, located close to Yoshida Shrine, was the former residence of Shinto priests. Four rocks placed next to a large, flat worship stone represent the Sennin Islands, believed in Chinese tradition to have been occupied by monks in possession of the elixir of life. This is the garden's central stone ensemble. The worship stone, or *raihai seki*, served as a place to stand in prayer while facing the direction of Yoshida Shrine. When Shigemori moved into the house in 1943, he redesigned the garden with the rock as its focal point.

Shigemori's trademark curved paving stones were an innovation in design that freed the paths and edges of gardens from the angled rigidity of the past. Here he used Tanba Kurama granite to create wave-shaped paving stones. These are set in a blend of cement and mortar mixed with *bengara*, a dark red pigment traditionally used to coat the wooden surfaces of homes. The cresting wave patterns create a sinuous movement that complements the garden's gravel surfaces, raked into lines suggestive of water.

Stepping stones, pebbles and humps of moss occupy the foreground space of the garden, while surprisingly large rocks feature in the middle ground. The background section consists of even larger stones and trees close to the rear wall. The largest of these rocks is thought to represent Mount Horai, the centre of the Buddhist cosmos.

At a relatively early point in his career, Shigemori recognized that 'the old is new'. He would later coin the expression 'eternal modern'[1] to describe the melding of the classical and contemporary in gardens, the notion that the traditional contains an exuberance that can invigorate the new.

1
With its healthy moss beds and well-raked gravel, the garden is meticulously maintained.

1

SHIGEMORI MIREI GARDEN MUSEUM

2
The *sekimori ishi*, or barrier stone, is an indication not to pass this point.

3
A typical, upward-thrusting Shigemori rock arrangement

4
Representations of islands, waves and mountains, traditional elements in a modern garden.

5 →
Shigemori's own residence garden contains many of the signature techniques and design features found in his other work.

2

3

6
A perfectly framed view from the main room of the residence.
7
Adjacent to the main building, a traditional teahouse.
8
A typical Shigemori convergence of stepping stones.

6

7

8

Ryoan-ji: Into the Mystic

The ancient garden of Ryoan-ji is a masterpiece of pure abstraction that looks strikingly contemporary. Trying to decode its mysteries, with only fourteen of its fifteen stones visible from any given angle, is the ultimate challenge for garden scholars.

Although Zen eschews exegesis, the garden encourages streams of theories, metaphorical interpretations and potential meanings. Are these rocks tiger cubs being led across a stream, islands in a grey sea or dark fragments of meteorites, so firmly embedded in gravel they have become symbols of immutability?

The dry landscape garden can never be dissociated from the metaphysical and intuitive faculties. Shigemori Mirei asserted that 'until you can silently meditate on it, until you can actually hear the sound of waves issuing from its entirety, you have not understood the garden at Ryoan-ji'.[1] Devotees of Zen claim that the sound of water can be heard at the moment of *satori*, or enlightenment, an assertion that may be actual or an auditory hallucination induced by a longing for religious ecstasy.

Awed by the durability of the garden, we stand before the composition, struggling to grasp its essence. 'The stone garden,' author Donald Richie wrote, 'is a moral object. It never answers questions, it only – like the sphinx – asks them.'[2]

115

Enigmatically, only fourteen of the garden's fifteen stones are visible at any one time.

PROJECT	**Kishiwada Castle Garden**
LOCATION	**Kishiki-cho, Kishiwada, Osaka Prefecture**
DESIGNER	**Shigemori Mirei**
YEAR	**1953**

116

Dominating the citadel-style courtyard of Kishiwada Castle, Shigemori Mirei's 1953 dry landscape garden has a suitably military theme. From the uppermost floor of the castle turret, we have a clear overview of his Hachi-jin no Niwa (Garden of Eight Combat Formations), the design representing a mythological Chinese battle, conducted by General Zhuge Liang.

The general's encampment, a dense cluster of rocks, stands at the centre of this generously proportioned 1,650-square-metre (17,760-square-foot) garden. The base is surrounded by eight protective sub-camps, auspiciously named Heaven, Earth, Wind, Cloud, Dragon, Tiger, Phoenix and Serpent. Peripheral groupings of rocks, consisting of between two and nine stones, are composed with Shigemori's preferred blue-tinged *aoishi*, or chlorite schist, extracted from the island of Okinoshima near Shikoku.

While in most Japanese gardens rectilinear geometry is confined to borders, here, raised stone lines occupy the inner spaces of the design scheme. Visitors are allowed to step onto these wall lines, similar to low ramparts, and explore the garden. Another way Shigemori sought to make the garden more accessible was by using the grounds for exhibitions and theatrical performances. Two years after it was completed, his daughter Yugo gave a dance performance on a stage erected there. The theme, appropriately, was the straight and curved line.

Shigemori's intention was that this singular garden could be viewed not only from the standard ground level or slight elevation afforded by a raised deck, but from a multitude of angles, including aerial perspectives from passing planes and helicopters.

1
Viewed from the upper turret of the castle, the layout of Shigemori's design is as clear as a chessboard.

1

KISHIWADA CASTLE GARDEN

2
Shigemori's unique synergy of military architecture and landscape design.
3
The stone groupings mirror the tough, assertively military theme of the garden.
4
In the arrangement of rocks, dynamism rather than beauty is the aim of the design.
5
The stone boundaries are sealed with concrete, almost like fortifications.

2

3

4

5

KISHIWADA CASTLE GARDEN

6
Shigemori's battlefield schemata is clearly visible from the castle turret.

6

KISHIWADA CASTLE GARDEN

PROJECT
LOCATION
DESIGNER
YEAR

Kagawa Prefectural Office
Bansho, Takamatsu, Kagawa Prefecture
Tange Kenzo
1958

When Tange Kenzo, Japan's first recipient of the prestigious Pritzker Architecture Prize, unveiled his 1958 Kagawa Prefectural Office structure and landscaped grounds, the line between contemporary garden design and architecture dissolved.

The pond garden fronting the central hall of the government building, with its strict, rectilinear parameters, faces a spacious, public plaza, which serves as a passageway for pedestrians and shoppers, and as a venue for open-air musical and theatrical performances. Water and stone reflect in the expansive glass panels of the entrance hall, creating a dynamic interplay of sculpted rock with the angled framework. The curving edges of a pond in the southern section of the plaza accentuate the ramrod-straight borders of the central water basin.

Significantly, the design represents the conscious transition from traditional garden to modern art, its stones shaped by the creator, rather than appropriated from nature. This shifts the garden away from being an arrangement of natural elements and moves it into the realm of sculptural composition.

Rock carving has existed in Japanese gardens for centuries, in the form of stone lanterns, pagodas, water basins, stepping stones, granite bridges, temple pillar pedestals and stones incised with Buddhist iconography, but Tange's creation represents the first time that rocks were cut into preconceived forms. Where traditional garden designers sought out the organic shapes of rocks found in the natural environmental, on mountainsides or in riverbeds, Tange opted to control the process, splitting locally sourced granite to assemble his forms into upright and fallen steles. There is still an element of happenstance here, as it is virtually impossible to know the exact forms they will assume once split.

It was highly unusual in the post-war years to find a project in which both buildings and garden were executed by the same hand. The large segments of rock look as if they could almost be unused fragments from the original office construction. This lends them an affinity with the buildings themselves, as if they could be re-inserted into the structure, perfectly coordinating in terms of colour and material.

The spatial infrastructure of the design is determined by the laws of geometry and the draughtsmanship of an architect, with very little left to chance. In Tange's seminal design, the curve becomes subservient to the right angle.

1
Irregular lines break up the rectilinear garden framing.

1

2

2
Sculptural forms perfectly match the garden's rock structure.
3
Rock placements create powerful upward angles.
4
Grass mounds help to soften the dominant presence of rock.
5
Tange Kenzo's innovative synergy of modern architecture and stone gardens.

3

4

5

6

7

6
The garden remains much the same as it was when constructed in the 1950s.
7
This shallow water pool is a later addition to the original design.
8
Flagstones and water lead to a small rock arrangement.

KAGAWA PREFECTURAL OFFICE

PROJECT

LOCATION

DESIGNER

YEAR

Kozen-ji
Fukushima, Kiso-machi
Shigemori Mirei
1963

128

A series of hedges beside the stone pathway leading to the entrance of Kozen-ji temple is pruned into undulating forms, creating patterns that, when replicated in the main garden, become almost kinetic.

Located in an ancient Kiso Valley post town on the trade and pilgrimage Nakasendo Road, the main garden of the Rinzai sect Zen temple was completed by landscape designer Shigemori Mirei in 1963. Strongly associated with Kyoto temple gardens, Shigemori wanted to experiment with a design that would reflect the natural environment outside of the garden walls. Inspired by the sea of clouds that gathers above the valley, his design, purportedly the largest gravel and sand garden in Japan, sits above the upper Kiso River at an altitude of 1,200 metres (3,937 feet). The garden, named Kanun-no-Niwa, the 'Garden for Appreciating Clouds', features a sinuous outline of cumulus represented by lines of white concrete snaking across gravel. 'I used a two-dimensional drawing technique,' Shigemori commented, 'for a garden which has three dimensions, something I have never seen done in a Japanese garden.'[1] A chequerboard patio, evoking the classic *ichi-matsu* pattern, divides the temple building from the principal, perfectly rectangular garden.

The cloud depiction, floating above a vast bed of gravel, contrasts with a 7–5–3 stone arrangement conforming with the Taoist concept of asymmetrical balance. The rocks, transported from the Seto Inland Sea, represent mountain peaks in an ocean of clouds, flaunting the traditional advice against creating clusters of upright rocks in close proximity.

Not a single plant, tree or blade of grass appeared in the original design. Frost and neglect have caused damage to the white concrete bands, and the branches of pine trees have been allowed to intrude into the garden. Shigemori, an advocate of spare compositions, would probably have objected to the resulting effect.

1
White lines segment the gravel into sub-areas of the garden.

1

2

3

2
Visitors view the garden from a chequered, *ichi-matsu*-patterned patio.

3
Tightly pruned hedges and embedded rocks at the entrance to the temple.

4
One of Shigemori Mirei's classic stone clusters.

4

KOZEN-JI

PROJECT
LOCATION

DESIGNER
YEAR

Yurin-no-Niwa
Kibichuo-cho, Kaga-gun, Okayama Prefecture
Shigemori Mirei
1969

132

Built as an adjoining feature to the exhibition hall of Kyoto's Association of Yuzen Manufacturers, the first incarnation of Shigemori Mirei's 1969 garden had a short life. In 1999, both the building and garden were demolished. Due to the timely intercession of Iwamoto Toshio, a former Shigemori apprentice, the dismantled garden components were reassembled in the courtyard of a newly constructed town hall in the designer's hometown of Kibichuo-cho in Okayama Prefecture.

The 'yu' in the name Yurin derives from Miyazaki Yuzensai, a prominent eighteenth-century master of the *yuzen* kimono silk dyeing technique. The 'rin' suffix is a dedication to the important Edo-era painter Ogata Korin. A modern version of the *chisen kanshoshiki teien*, a pond appreciation garden, Yurin-no-niwa is one of Shigemori's most abstract designs. The work differs from many of his other gardens in its emphasis on a detailed, largely water-submerged horizontal plain, with only a minimal number of the artist's signature vertical rocks. Two hewn stone spirals weave across interconnecting beds of red and blue stones, accessed respectively from the Kyoto prefectural district of Tamba and the island of Shikoku. Pond borders and paving allow viewers to access the design and alter their perspective. Open to the general public, the third floor of the town hall office affords a drawing board view of the entire garden.

Deep in the Okayama countryside, and with an irregular bus service, the location means the work is viewed by only a limited number of public office workers, locals and the occasional garden researcher.

1
Water gently circulates and exits the garden.

1

YURIN-NO-NIWA

2

3

2
A rock island placed among the swirling lines of the garden.
3
Stone spirals placed beside angled lines create an interesting tension.
4
The second-floor view of the garden helps to clarify Shigemori's design.

4

YURIN-NO-NIWA

Kengo Kuma

136

Japanese Gardens and Modernism

1

ESSAY: KENGO KUMA

2

The German architect Bruno Taut has been credited with the 'rediscovery' of the Katsura Rikyu Imperial Villa in Kyoto, considered the most complete among the numerous traditional gardens designed in Japan. Taut already had considerable interest in gardens before his stay in Japan. Critical of Formalism and the supremacy of architectural form found in the architecture of his contemporaries Le Corbusier and Mies van der Rohe, he had explored new forms of architecture that were integrated with the environment. In contrast to their hard, man-made architecture, the ideal city envisioned in Taut's environmental manifesto *Alpine Architektur* (1919) is a crystalline city in harmony with the alpine mountain ranges.

However, Taut's ideas were at odds with the emphasis on man-made objects in Europe. There was a flourishing discourse on their design, but nature was positioned as their polar opposite and methodologies for designing nature were extremely immature. This was in contrast to Japan, where ideas about how to create nature had been thoroughly studied and tested since the *Sakutei-ki*.

Surrounded as he was by a Western framework focused on man-made objects, it makes sense that Taut felt no attraction to Western garden discourse. The geometric French garden was merely an extension into the garden of the Formalism he had rejected. The English landscape garden was the antithesis of the geometric garden, but it was no more than a vague presence outside architecture and design. Taut was craving a kind of comprehensive theory that did not exist in the West, one that covered the whole environment around people and connected architecture with nature.

Taut's discovery of a new environmental theory when he encountered Japanese gardens feels inevitable. It is said that he was moved to tears when he first saw the Katsura Rikyu Imperial Villa. In his notes, he describes the encounter as the best birthday present of his life. As it turned out, a small island in the distant East concealed something that he had spent a lifetime searching for and never finding in the West.

Aside from its profound influence on garden design in Japan, the *Sakutei-ki*, compiled in Japan in the latter half of the eleventh century, is also thought to be the oldest text on garden design anywhere in the world. Even the modern reader is dazzled by the breadth and quality of the text, which covers the philosophy, principles and spirituality of gardens as well as specific discussions of technique.

There are surprisingly few comparable books discussing architecture in Japan. The *Kiwarisho*, a technical manual compiled in the Edo period, was widely read among craftsmen. It is sometimes referred to as a forerunner of Le Corbusier's modular theory, but it contains no discussion of the philosophy or principles of architecture at all. Rather, the text is a record of the standard dimensions of all components for wooden buildings.

Quite the opposite is true in the West, where discourse on architecture has been dominant since the Roman engineer Vitruvius wrote his treatise on the discipline, whereas discourse on gardens has been negligible. This is by no means to suggest that Japanese architecture was of a low standard in comparison to the high standard of Japanese gardens. In Japan, architecture was considered subordinate to gardens, and buildings were never required to have a prominent presence in the garden. Architecture had to be unobtrusive to avoid disturbing the rhythm and flow of the garden. The *Sakutei-ki* provided the overarching environmental theory, while the true meaning of the *Kiwarisho* was to establish a system of permitted dimensions for architecture. As long as these were observed, the aesthetic order of the environment as a whole, including gardens and architecture, was maintained. So comprehensive was the philosophy of the *Sakutei-ki* that gardens always took precedence over architecture.

1
The Katsura Rikyu Imperial Villa is an exercise in sublime simplicity.

2
Natural, pruned and rectilinear lines meet in a section of the Katsura Rikyu Imperial Villa.

Taut recorded his thoughts on the encounter in several accounts. Most strikingly, he points out that although the Katsura Rikyu Imperial Villa was for the use of the royal family, the architecture resembled crudely built barracks, by Western standards. He observes that it is the sense of unity and continuity between the garden and the architecture that people find deeply moving, indicating that beauty does not lie in the object itself, but in relationships.

It was not simply a beautiful garden he discovered at Katsura, but a completely different design philosophy to replace the architecture-centric design logic of Modernism. One that regarded architecture and garden, architecture and the environment as a single organic continuum. It was a new environmental design theory and a new methodology for global design, anticipating a time when the Earth's environment would be confronted with a crisis.

Bruno Taut died in Turkey five years after the encounter with the Katsura Rikyu Imperial Villa. Five years was too short a time to practise and develop a new environmental design discourse. Then, not long afterwards, the Second World War broke out and his discovery was forgotten. Taut's design discourse was prophetic, but in the end, never completed.

When Walter Gropius visited Japan for the first time in 1954, he was also astonished and full of praise for the Katsura Rikyu Imperial Villa, describing its simplicity as the pinnacle of beauty. However, unlike Taut, Gropius did not direct his praise at the garden, but exclusively at the architecture. Shortly after Gropius's post-war visit, Japan was racing towards reconstruction and rapid growth, and there was no longer any leeway to pay attention to gardens. Gropius was the perfect advisor for post-war Japan, where the overriding objective was to faithfully follow the Modernist aesthetic to provide large quantities of simple buildings at low cost. Although acclaimed worldwide, *KATSURA: Tradition and Creation in Japanese Architecture* (1960), a book with text by Gropius and Tange Kenzo, mainly discussed the simple and functional architecture and said very little about the garden. Ishimoto Yasuhiro, who took the photographs, even trimmed and cropped the roofs, which are the most important elements of the architecture at Katsura, sacrificing them to a Modernist theory that disliked pitched roofs.

Japan sacrificed its beautiful environment and its beautiful gardens in exchange for economic growth. Only gardens can rescue us from the resulting desolate landscape that we now see before us. To revive the garden, we need a comprehensive, global environmental discourse focused on gardens. For Japanese people, a garden was never just a garden; it was always connected to the universe and it taught us universal truths. Now, more than ever, when the planet is on the verge of crisis, we must focus on gardens, and by extension, the Earth and the universe.

3

3
A small tatami mat room acts as a viewing platform at the Katsura Rikyu Imperial Villa.

4
With its central pond and circulating paths, the Katsura Rikyu Imperial Villa is a prototype for the Japanese stroll garden.

5
A rich concentration of variegated greenery at the Katsura Rikyu Imperial Villa.

4

5

PROJECT

Rinsho-ji

LOCATION

Shindachiokanaka, Sennan-shi, Osaka Prefecture

DESIGNER

Shigemori Mirei

Although Shigemori Mirei is strongly associated with the Kansai region, which includes the great cities of Kyoto, Nara and Osaka, one occasionally comes across one of his landscapes in a remote rural area, distinctive works forgotten by the garden fraternity because of their remoteness. The Rinsho-ji temple garden, a highly pictorial creation deep in the Osaka countryside, is one such site.

A large space was needed to create the multi-level design, which resembles an elevated, slightly tilted English knot garden or maze. Shadowy blocks spill like dark, liquid light into the spaces between large segments of azalea bushes, creating an irregular green and black chequered effect, with wedges of shade suspended like a sequence of dark pools.

Shigemori's early training in landscape ink and wash painting, flower arrangement and the tea ceremony strongly influenced his sense of garden composition, particularly in the spare arrangements of the stone garden. Here, the natural landscape lends itself to his design, rendered in a tiered, perennial greenery. Starkly contrasting with much of his work in the dry landscape field, the design reflects the influence of the topiary master, poet and aristocrat Enshu Kobori (1579–1647), as can be seen in the stacked, graduated hedges, each portion perfectly interlocking. Narrow pathways snake behind each block, invisible from the front, their purpose to provide access for pruning and weeding. The warm, curving geometry is firmly within the traditions of Japanese garden typology but with a contemporary audacity of scale; its wave patterns replicate those used in Japanese kimono design.

A Modernist gifted with traditional garden-making skills, Shigemori believed that innovation should remain culturally grounded. This theory closely aligned him with the ideas of Japan's Primitive Modern movement, an approach supported by architects and artists including Tange Kenzo, Noguchi Isamu and Takiguchi Shuzo.

1
Shigemori Mirei's trademark vertical stones soar out of the hedges.

1

2
One of the pleasures of the garden is ascending its paths and gaining different perspectives.

3
The atypical lushness of this Shigemori Mirei garden evokes a Buddhist vision of Nirvana.

2

3

4
A gurgling water source adds much needed refreshment, especially in the humid summer months.

4

PROJECT

LOCATION

DESIGNER

YEAR

Sekizo-ji
Ichijima-cho, Hikami-gun, Hyogo Prefecture
Shigemori Mirei
1972

146

Considering its rural location, the temple garden of Sekizo-ji is both remarkably well maintained and assertively modern.

Completed in 1972, this late Shigemori Mirei work departs from the formal stone garden approach of using rocks to recreate mythological landscapes, opting instead for single symbolic arrangements. Another striking innovation is the use of four contrasting colours of gravel, where for centuries, one sufficed.

If first impressions are of a highly contemporary layout, the underlying design principles dig deep into Chinese religious philosophy and geomancy, resulting in what garden writer Christian Tschumi contends is the 'first garden in Japan ever to be based on the concept of *shishin soo*'.[1] This refers to a quartet of gods who protect the four divine directions. Each god is represented by rock settings facing the temple's main hall.

The east arrangement, emblematic of the dragon, or earth guardian, is linked to the colour blue. Accordingly, long stones representing the Blue Dragon are placed in the east section of the garden and surrounded with matching blue gravel. A similar colour association is visible in the southern corner of the garden, where striated scarlet stones represent the Red Phoenix. This mythological creature, symbolizing the element of fire, sits on a bed of red sand resembling an outcrop of rocks on the planet Mars. The White Tiger, representing the element of metal, occupies the west portion of the garden, the stone setting surrounded by a bed of white gravel. The dark, rocky features of a tortoise, the water guardian, stand to the north, embedded in an expanse of black volcanic sand.

Visible in high relief on the surface of bamboo fencing, *kanji*, or Chinese characters, run along parts of the garden border. Leached of colour, the grey strokes of the characters, looking like mystic runes to the illiterate, read *shishin* and *seki*, the latter referencing the first ideogram of the temple's name.

A network of paths, each with its own stone patterning, slices the garden into four sections. These allow visitors to enter and interact with the garden, rather than observing it from a raised deck, the customary arrangement with dry landscape gardens.

Given the huge importance of this design in the development of the Japanese stone garden, Shigemori's daring work at Sekizo-ji deserves considerably more attention than it receives. It seems that the remote location has condemned the garden to an unintended obscurity.

1
Using different-coloured gravel was a groundbreaking innovation.

1

2

2
Exposed moss needs regular watering to save it from withering.
3
An unusual rock formation with a gravel bed of straight lines.
4
A careful combination of flat and upright stone arrangements.
5
A visually stimulating compression of stone pathways and gravel.

3

4

5

PROJECT

LOCATION

DESIGNER

YEAR

Fukuchi-in
Koya-san, Ito-gun, Wakayama Prefecture
Shigemori Mirei
1975

The temple-strewn summit of Mount Koya, in the wooded depths of Wakayama Prefecture, is one of Japan's most sacred spots. Fukuchi-in is a well-known *shukubo*, or temple lodging, of which there are over forty on the mountain.

Visitors are invited to participate in morning ceremonies and meditation sessions, and to sample its vegetarian cuisine. The premises are comfortable, even opulent, but still feel, in the manner of a mendicant monk's modest abode, like a place of material privation and spiritual promise. Aside from the experience of lodging overnight in a Buddhist temple, garden scholars and enthusiasts stay here to appreciate its inner gardens, designed by iconoclast Shigemori Mirei.

Two of the three gardens at Fukuchi-in are only accessible to guests. Completed in 1975, the gardens consist of an outer dry landscape, crisscrossed by a curved and diagonal path, forming a fluid grid. According to Shigemori's son Kanto, this garden, visible on the approach to the temple, represents the 'solemnity of Buddhism' combined with references to indigenous Shinto.

Viewed from a lobby within the temple itself are two inner designs of great interest. One is another dry landscape garden, with contrasting coloured gravel and a sinuous, pebble-like containing path made from tile. The overall effect, a very dramatic one, is of a stream meandering through a landscape of erupting rocks. The elevation of materials to the spiritual or transcendental realm is achieved by the simple device of giving the space a name, in this instance Yusen-tei, meaning 'Paradise Garden'. According to garden writer Christian Tschumi, Shigemori saw this as the place where 'the human soul would go to play and seek the truth'.[1]

An adjacent pond garden, with a curving backdrop of azalea bushes, seemingly representing billowing seas, mountains and hills, rises into an imagined infinity of space. This may explain the name of this unique design: Tosen-tei, meaning 'Ascending to Paradise Garden'. Symbolizing the idea of longevity, a stone arrangement on a small island in the middle of the pond features a tortoise and crane grouping, a common pairing in traditional gardens. The landscapes are impeccably maintained.

Shigemori had passed away by the time the garden was completed with the aid of his long-serving construction chief, Okamoto Yukio. The final work remains a fitting coda to a landscaping career inspired by Buddhist principles, deeply intuited cultural considerations and a powerful yearning for Modernism.

1
The garden incorporates a number of small symbolic islands.

1

2

3

2
The use of coloured gravel was highly innovative.

3
Tiles sealed with red mortar contrast with the coloured gravel.

4
Part of a temple that offers overnight stays to visitors, the gardens are meticulously well maintained.

4

FUKUCHI-IN

5
Shigemori Mirei favoured upright stones over the horizontal.

5

FUKUCHI-IN

6

6
Flowing hills and sinuous pond embankments complement each other.

7
A carp glides around the only water spot in the temple gardens.

8
The temple's front garden resorts to more traditional garden forms for its effects.

7 

 8

PROJECT	**Matsuo Taisha**
LOCATION	**Nishikyo-ku, Kyoto**
DESIGNER	**Shigemori Mirei**
YEAR	**1975**

158

The gardens at the water deity shrine of Matsuo Taisha were Shigemori Mirei's last project. Completed in 1975, the first landscape in the trilogy, the Horai Garden, consists of a number of islets floating in a shallow, phoenix-shaped pond, a depiction of the ancient Chinese concept of paradise, the Islands of the Immortals. The garden is atypical for Shigemori, as it uses real water instead of his preferred abstracted version, made from sand and gravel.

The inner landscape, the Kyokusui no Niwa, or Garden of the Winding Stream, is the most contemporary of the set. The shallow brook that flows through the garden is a natural stream, but its banks and bed are made from blue rocks cut into flat paving stones set in concrete. In the Heian era (794–1185), garden streams were created not only as decorative elements, but for members of the nobility to entertain themselves by sending cups of sake down the currents, composing a single line of a verse that would be expanded by the next person to pick up the vessel. Undulating streams of this type are also associated with doll-floating events, in which paper models are sent down the meandering waterway in the belief that they will take evil spirits with them.

The backdrop to the stream is an undulating mass of topiary, tightly clipped azalea bushes pierced by soaring rocks. Assertively modern, the composition pays tribute to traditional garden associations, its configuration the shape of a turtle, a symbol of longevity. The deliberate absence of trees allows light to suffuse the garden in every season.

The Joko no Niwa, or Prehistoric Garden, sees Shigemori returning to the pre-Shinto origins of the Japanese garden, the powerful rock arrangement evoking the aura of an *iwakura*, a gathering place for the gods. Shigemori believed that sacred rocks, and the devotion accorded them, were the origin of the Japanese garden. Inspired by a natural rock standing on the mountain behind the shrine, one honoured as a deity, Shigemori, in his final garden, aspired towards the divine.

The further the garden climbs, the stronger its rock arrangements become. The large upper-layer rocks, weighing between five and eight tons each and placed at opposing angles, are made from blue schist from Shikoku Island, Shigemori's favourite stone. Standing amidst bamboo grass, this almost Palaeolithic rock grouping, devoid of all ornamentation, returns the designer to the roots of his devotion to the Japanese garden.

1
Shigemori Mirei's use of azalea bushes helps to soften the impact of rock, concrete and tile.

1

MATSUO TAISHA

2

2
The meandering stream draws its water from the mountain behind the shrine.

3
Shigemori returned to the sacred rock origins in this final garden.

3

MATSUO TAISHA

4

5

4
One of the rare times Shigemori used actual water, rather than symbolic water, in a garden.

5
A mini landscape within the garden.

Sonic Layers

When the plum rains descended in China, poets would gather under the shelter of garden pergolas and pavilions to listen to the sound of water dripping from the eaves, a custom Japanese aestheticians adopted, alongside practices like listening to the song of insects, distant temple bells or the sawing of wind through pine trees.

For the people of Edo (Tokyo), a popular seasonal amusement was to seek out the grassy plain on the city's edge, a riverbank or a garden for *mushi-kiki*, the pleasures of listening to singing insects. Set free into bushes, their sounds were savoured in the early autumn night. *Suzumushi* (*Homoeogryllus japonicus*) and *kutsuwa-mushi* (bush crickets) were among the insects favoured. So too were *kajika*, singing frogs from garden ponds.

Each garden possessed a singular sound topography. Ogawa Jihei's (1860–1933) gardens were distinctive for his skill in creating soundscapes through the careful placing of waterfalls and purling brooks. In the *chisen*, or pond garden, the movement of water creates sound. Bamboo was planted partly for its aesthetic appeal, but also for the hollow, woody sound it made when the wind induced trunks to gently collide.

A partly functional, partly ornamental feature of traditional Japanese gardens is the *shishi odoshi*, or 'deer scarer'. Water flows into a cut bamboo rod. When the channel is full, it overflows, releasing the section of trunk onto a stone. This emits a crisp, pleasing clack, a hollow resonance recalling the percussive effects used in Noh dramas.

Another interesting auditory installation from the Edo era, the *suikinkutsu*, is a device that emits a soothing sound as water drips from a stone laver, through the earth, into a buried ceramic jar, audible via a bamboo pipe. It is one of those aesthetic refinements that, cleansing body and mind, also functions as a simple novelty item adding to the garden soundscape.

When the climate is sultry or oppressive, which it invariably is during the Japanese rainy season, water is welcomed for its cleansing and refreshing qualities, but also its audio effects. Neuroscience suggests the sound of running water can evoke or unlock pleasant memories from the past. During this season, *kusaridoi*, or rain chains, produce another pleasing sound effect. A feature of both temple and private gardens, *kusaridoi* function as a vertical gutter, conveying water as it gushes off rooftops.

Adding to the soundscapes of temple gardens are bells, gongs and the muted chanting of sutras from ordination halls. Genyu-en, a stroll garden in Hikone with a *shakkei* (borrowed view) of the town's castle, is the setting for an engaging audio experience. The citadel's time-keeping bell and the chirping of cicadas and crickets in the garden were included as one of the 100 Soundscapes of Japan, a listing compiled by the Ministry of the Environment to combat noise pollution and enhance the environment.

In modern urban gardens, however, the sonic landscape – random, fluid, disruptive – is likely to be more distracting than soothing.

During heavy rain, water pours down a *kusaridoi* (rain chain), creating an aesthetically pleasing soundtrack to the garden.

PROJECT
LOCATION
DESIGNER
YEAR

Kyoto International Conference Center
Takaragaike, Sakyo-ku, Kyoto
Otani Sachio / Komatsu Toshiro
1966

164

With its own dedicated subway station on the northern edge of Kyoto, at first glance the massive hulk of the conference centre, constructed in 1966, evokes a Cold War-era Soviet silo, or an example of the Brutalist school of architecture that originated in Britain in the 1950s. A kinder and more informed interpretation came from the creator himself, Otani Sachio (1924–2013), who likened the design, with its combined, reversed trapezoid shapes, to vernacular *gassho zukuri* residences, soaring three- and four-floor rural homes with roofs that imitate the shape of praying hands.

The generous grounds include a 23,000-square-metre (247,570-square-foot) stroll garden overlooking a geometrically patterned pond, crisscrossed by a modern concrete version of the raised eight-planked *yatsuhashi* bridges found in traditional landscape designs. The garden acts as a transitional space between a natural backdrop of hills and the geometric megastructure of the conference hall.

Kyoto-based Ueyakato Landscape were commissioned to construct the New Hall in 2018, with the theme of 'garden and architecture as one'. Created by landscape designer Komatsu Toshiro, to include a courtyard, a dry landscape and an inner reception garden, the concept was tested in the preliminary stages in collaboration with Ueyakato Landscape, using sample mock-ups. The New Hall restores us to a familiar contemporary Japanese garden world of greenery encased in treated concrete, the garden as lightwell and spatial interlude.

1
Walkways inside the New Hall are open and exposed to this rock garden arrangement.

1

KYOTO INTERNATIONAL CONFERENCE CENTER

2

3

2
Powerful boulders compete with the machine part-influenced architecture of the centre.
3
The designer has tried to soften the effect of concrete with ambient plantings.
4
Beds of rock fragments are softened by proximity to grass and small trees.
5
Zig-zag bridges in the landscaped garden evoke earlier forms.
6 →
The garden pond contrasts with the assertive 1960s structures.

4

5

7

7
Open-air garden galleries along the New Hall.

8
Configurated in the shape of a horizontal scroll, this garden gallery also acts as a light well.

8

PROJECT

LOCATION

DESIGNER

YEAR

Adachi Museum of Art
Furukawa-cho, Yasugi, Shimane Prefecture
Nakane Kinsaku
1970

172

Designed by Nakane Kinsaku (1917–1995), in close consultation with the museum's owner, Adachi Zenko (1899–1990), a wealthy business magnate and art collector, this superlative dry landscape embraces such exacting aesthetic standards that it risks upstaging the impressive collection of paintings and ceramics housed here.

Nakane, a highly influential force in modern landscaping, considered this his most important commission. Completed in 1970, the interconnecting gardens, a modern masterpiece, are designed for contemplation and reflection, rather than strolling. The museum grounds are divided into five main zones: a dry landscape garden, a white gravel garden, a pine garden, a moss garden and a pond garden. The grounds cover a staggering 43,000 square metres (462,848 square feet).

There is nothing random about the elements of this well-contoured space. The design sustains visual attention by constantly altering scale and perspective. Topiary is used here to create a deliberate optical effect of depth, while the use of large rocks and clipped forms at the front of the view brings the foreground closer to the observer, making the middle and background spaces appear smaller and more distant.

In Nakane's white gravel and black pine gardens, colour is reduced to a restricted palette of evergreen azaleas and Japanese red and black pines. The tightly grouped Satsuki azaleas are shaped into hemispheres and, with the carefully composed rock settings, positioned on a graduated slope. A picturesque waterfall, the focal point of this carefully managed perspective, appears at the apex of the triangle formed by the rock and plant placements. A compelling visual focus skilfully unifying the design, the cascade turns out, in a rather contemporary utilitarian manner, to be artificial. The managed compression of space artfully conceals the busy road that exists just beyond the row of pines.

One of the necessary restrictions of the dry landscape garden is that, with very few exceptions, visitors are not permitted to enter the composition. The design of the museum galleries and corridors helps to compensate for the restricted perspectives. Broad windows and apertures frame painterly landscapes as visitors proceed through the galleries, with each section of the garden appearing in differently framed segments. Observed from inside the building, the wall openings are flanked by works from the museum's collection, creating a seamless integration of art, architecture and landscape.

In Nakane's work we recognize that the modern Japanese garden is a free form of art. Rather than simply creating a composition in the service of art, however, the Adachi gardens embody the search for the essence of landscape, the ultimate purpose of all Japanese gardens.

1
Clipping and pruning the pines and hedges requires a permanent team of gardeners.

1

ADACHI MUSEUM OF ART

2
A busy foreground, but the garden also manages to incorporate a borrowed view.

2

3

3
A masterful synergy of natural landscape and garden design.

4
The tranquil Japanese tearoom is reached via a narrow stone path.

5
An open porch allows visitors to step out and breathe in the air of the gardens.

4

5

PROJECT
LOCATION

DESIGNER
YEAR

Shonandai Cultural Center
Shonandai, Fujisawa City, Kanagawa prefecture
Hasegawa Itsuko
1990

At its most radical, the modern meta-garden dispenses entirely with natural elements. The Shonandai Cultural Center, which includes a children's museum, civic theatre and planetarium, is an example of an entirely fabricated landscape, whose only natural component is water. Its creator, architect Hasegawa Itsuko, defines the composition's mash of plaza pools, pyramidal roofs, spheres and an undulating stream as 'another nature'.

Hasegawa has talked about the 'liquidity and diversity' of her sites, of the process of planning and conceiving architecture as a 'work of making topography'.[1] That fluidity and inclusion of landscape contouring are evident in the combination of elements such as silvery surfaces, cage-like panels of steel, perforated aluminium trees, a riverbed made from tile, stained glass, vine-hung stainless-steel pergolas and a set of cosmic spheres.

Hasegawa was the first woman to win an architectural competition of this type, and reactions among the older male fraternity of Japanese designers were less than flattering, with one well-known architect comparing her plan to a 'naïve child's drawing' and another deriding it as 'gaudy, pop, idiosyncratic and eccentric'.[2] There are certainly playful elements in the design, with seashells embedded in its floors and concrete walls, tiles embossed with animal tracks and green and blue marbles placed above perforated ceiling panels. This is a garden very much within the public domain, When its winding stream, made from artificial tiles, is filled with water, children magically appear to paddle and play, creating the atmosphere of a fairytale village in the midst of a cluttered urban residential zone. Unbeknown to the gambolling toddlers, the *yari-mizu*, or winding stream, is an ancient garden component.

The completion of the project was a small but significant triumph over gender discrimination. Hasegawa recalls male local officials treating her 'as if I were a radical social activist'.[3] She recalled that the local bureaucrat assigned to supervise the project felt that 'like the sumo wrestling ring, women should not be allowed to enter a construction site'. Hasegawa prevailed and the project was completed in 1990.

The absence of natural materials does not appear to have diminished the popularity of the site, or its recognition by locals as a garden. This raises some interesting questions. If the unstated intention of the contemporary landscape artist is to create a Modernist utopia, a futuristic garden prototype, is it possible to do so by means of purely synthetic materials?

1
Even without water, the stream seems to flow.

1

2

2
The only concession to natural elements is the centre's narrow stream.

3
Made from manufactured materials, the water course is based on winding streams in ancient Heian-era gardens.

3

4

4
The stream consists of a complex interlocking of tiles.
5
Tightly gridded tiles create a sense of movement.
6
Stainless steel rods and perforated palm leaves add to the deliberate artificiality of the garden.
7
In the warmer months, the synthetic stream is filled with water for children to paddle in.

5

7

6

PROJECT

LOCATION

DESIGNER

YEAR

Canadian Embassy
3–38 Akasaka, Minato-ku
Masuno Shunmyo
1991

In accord with Shigemori Mirei's concept of the 'eternal modern', the work of Masuno Shunmyo straddles eras with the assurance of a master. A good example of his strikingly original approach is the 1991 Canadian Embassy stone garden in Tokyo's Aoyama-itchome district, regarded by many as a modern masterpiece.

Given that priests were once employed as stone setters in gardens, it is perhaps not surprising that innovative contemporary garden designer Masuno, who was head priest of a Soto Zen temple in Yokohama, holds that making a garden, even the most radically modern one, is the equivalent of spiritual training.

In this highly contemporary garden, rocks and boulders, set across a fourth-floor terrace with a cantilevered roof and a sweeping *shakkei* (borrowed view) of Akasaka Palace and its verdant treetops, are infused with an extraordinary sense of lightness and fluidity. The powerful combination of raw and cut granite has been arranged to represent the Canadian Shield, with a row of contrasting polished pyramidal forms replicating the Rocky Mountains. The roughly cut edges and wedge holes of the stones have been left intact, revealing process and human intervention, while the larger rocks have been hollowed out to lessen their weight, a method unheard of in traditional gardens. But then, you would be hard pressed to find an ancient landscape garden cantilevered over the upper storey of a modern building.

Symbolizing Japan, a smaller, more introspective garden, with more discernible traditional features, such as raked sand, a curving bamboo fence, a stone *nobedan* walkway and skilfully configured *tateishi* (standing stones), occupies a corner of the western section.

One wonders about the future of urban landscapes in Japanese cities, which are notorious for their scrap and build, rapid replacement approach to construction. Will gardens of the future be portable structures, readily dismantled, then reassembled in fresh locations like art installations?

When asked how he felt about the use of easily replaceable materials such as carbon fibre, concrete and translucent polycarbonate in some modern Japanese gardens, Masuno responded, 'The first thing to consider when creating a modern Japanese garden is whether the material will retain its presence for hundreds of years. I prefer not to use materials that cannot guarantee this.'[1]

1
Many consider Masuno Shunmyo's Canadian Embassy design a modern masterpiece.

1

CANADIAN EMBASSY

2

2
Autumn light changes the way the garden is both illuminated and perceived.

3
Flat and sloping rocks engage harmoniously with a plain of fractured stones.

187

3

CANADIAN EMBASSY

4

5

6

4
Interlocking surfaces create a firmly bolted-down garden surface.

5
An aquatic section of the garden overlooks the Akasaka Palace grounds.

6
Sculptural forms add interest to the water garden.

8

7

7
Raked sand and a *nobedan* pathway hint at older garden elements.

8
A dramatically split standing stone immediately engages the eye.

PROJECT

National Institute for Materials Science (Fuma Byakuren Plaza)

LOCATION

Sengen, Tsukuba City, Ibaraki Prefecture

DESIGNER

Masuno Shunmyo

YEAR

1993

At first glance, the Fuma Byakuren Plaza, one of Japan's largest dry landscape gardens, resembles an unfinished excavation site, a plain of unearthed masonries. Masuno Shunmyo, the designer of this 1993 garden, said he drew inspiration from humankind's first encounter with metals. With little greenery or other natural growth, the water-deprived garden is intended to evoke the setting experienced by early gold prospectors, who encountered nature as a hostile, resistant force.

With rare exceptions, our viewpoint in stone gardens is almost always fixed, restricted to an observation deck that permits a single compositional framing. In this garden, however, we find human forms moving amidst the sculpted rocks. Administrative staff and researchers in white uniforms, random figures in a calculated landscape. The institute requested that the garden be practical and usable, so it provides space for workers to gather and discuss their work in an informal manner. As they move around inside the garden, the design recomposes itself.

Referencing Heian-era features, Masuno has threaded a *kyokusui*, or winding brook, through the garden, a dry stream strewn with nuggets of rock. The stream widens and contracts, scoping out a route between rocks representing mountains. It bores through a landscape that creates the illusion of being formed by wind, rain and erosion. The serpentine flow of the dry river exerts a seemingly magnetic force on the rocks in the garden, inducing them to face the same downstream direction, an effect creating harmony among an irregularity of forms.

Curving lines and natural contours contrast with the flat surfaces of the buildings. Architectural simplicity and mundanity are placed against the complexity of rocks erupting between a complex, geometrical layering of horizontal paving stones. These exposed rocks are presented as evidence of geological time, the natural changes in the earth itself. The fragmented edges and rough surfaces of the rocks reveal, in some instances, drill and chisel marks, indicating human intervention and the quarried origin of the material.

Harmonizing the rational nature of science and intuitive design with his own spiritual grounding as a Zen priest, Masuno has described himself as a devotee of Soseki Muso (1275–1351), a monk and seminal garden designer, who believed that the spiritual world inhabited all living matter, that 'in the garden, we might discover Buddha nature in all things'.[1]

Like his ancient mentor, Masuno views garden-making as a form of spiritual training, a perspective that allows him to create a landscape for an organization that, even in its name, stridently declares its materiality.

1
A complex scheme of flagstones and embedded rocks.

1

NATIONAL INSTITUTE FOR MATERIALS SCIENCE (FUMA BYAKUREN PLAZA)

2
Chiselled rock edges left to indicate the hand of the craftsman.

3
Natural rocks have been carved and shaped in the manner of sculpture.

4
A view of Masuno's winding stream from an upper floor of the institute.

2

3

4

NATIONAL INSTITUTE FOR MATERIALS SCIENCE (FUMA BYAKUREN PLAZA)

5

5
Workers from the research centre can freely move through the garden.

6
Powerful rock clusters placed at strategic positions throughout the garden.

7
Grass and a limited number of trees provide welcome smidgens of greenery.

6

7

NATIONAL INSTITUTE FOR MATERIALS SCIENCE (FUMA BYAKUREN PLAZA)

Masono Shunmyo

198 Japanese Gardens and Architectural Form

1

ESSAY: MASUNO SHUNMYO

2

For many years, Japanese culture has been focused on how to make nature palpable and how to create living spaces at one with nature. For this reason, nature, in the form of gardens, has been seen as a space that is one with the building. Traditional Japanese buildings use natural materials such as wood, earth and paper, but it has become rare to see such buildings in today's urban areas. Since the period of high economic growth, large buildings and even homes have mainly been made of steel, concrete and glass. In this context, the core materials that used to make up Japanese gardens are no longer suitable for certain buildings, due to the expansion of the scale of buildings and the change in the texture of the materials that make up the buildings themselves. A mismatch between modern architecture and Japanese gardens has arisen. Everyone thought that Japanese gardens no longer fit modern architecture, and no one tried to bring the Japanese garden and its ideas into that space during this period of architectural transformation.

However, looking at Japanese gardens historically, they have changed with the times as people's lifestyles and architectural styles have changed. For example, the *shinden-zukuri* style (an architectural style of associated with residences of the nobility) of the Heian period changed to the *shoin-zukuri* style (the drawing room or study style) in the Kamakura and Muromachi periods, and then to the *sukiya-zukuri* style (Japanese tearoom style) in the Momoyama period. Naturally, the way the gardens were designed also changed, reflecting the architectural styles and lifestyles of that period. In the post-war era, as buildings and people's lifestyles rapidly modernized and internationalized, Japanese gardens failed to respond to the trends and stagnated for a long time. However, having been devoted to Japanese garden design since before 1990, I had long been searching for a way to revive Japanese gardens that would fit in with contemporary architecture and urban spaces. The core is the 'Zen Garden'. I am still active in this field today and have created over 100 works around the world. Of these, the representative works in Tokyo include the garden of the Cerulean Tower Tokyu Hotel near Shibuya Station, the garden of the Hotel Le Port in Kojimachi, the Canadian Embassy garden and the courtyard of the Ministry of Foreign Affairs. In particular, the Cerulean Tower Tokyu Hotel, completed in 2001, gave me an opportunity to realize in the present space the idea of integrating and enhancing exterior and interior spaces, which is a characteristic of Japanese spatial construction. In this project, the design elements of the exterior space were incorporated into the interior space, and the garden and the interior lobby lounge were integrated as a unified whole. This design concept also extended to the hotel's front and reception. The Cerulean Tower Tokyu Hotel is a high-rise building constructed with modern materials. Therefore, instead of using traditional moss-covered stones, I used granite with a sharper texture for the garden and the lobby lounge.

This kind of approach, fusing the garden and interior, is still applied in many projects today. Currently, I am involved in a large number of overseas projects, and in many cases I also design interior spaces that are closely related to gardens. The regions covered range from Japan, Europe and Asia to North America. These philosophies, inherited from traditional Japanese garden design principles, are still alive today.

The fundamentals of my designs are, needless to say, the values and aesthetic sense that are unique to Japan, which is unlikely to change, regardless of how the times and our lifestyles change. Paradoxically, this aesthetic is in fact about a beauty that never stops changing, like the light interweaving with shadow, the water reflecting the scenery of masonry and trees, and the birds chirping, all of which are brought together and treated as carefully as possible. When maple trees are planted in a garden, the branches sway in the wind, showing a transient beauty. Japanese people find unspeakable grace in the way that greenery is reflected on the surface of water, or the manner in which shadows are cast on moss. It is beautiful because of its very impermanence, just like the falling of leaves from a deciduous tree. Here, I have used maple leaves as an example for ease of understanding, but this way of thinking should permeate every corner of the space. This is the beauty of Japan. I believe that applying this aesthetic sense and these values to urban Japanese gardens is a way of passing on Japanese culture. Since the 1990s, this has led to Japan being recognized across the world, and I have had the honour of receiving project requests from many countries.

1
Highly visible from the fourth-floor reception level, the Canadian Embassy garden is discreetly concealed from street view.

2
The landscape design at the National Institute for Materials Science garden successfully resolves oppositional forms.

PROJECT

LOCATION

DESIGNER

YEAR

Carbon Fibre Garden
Ariake, Koto-ku, Tokyo
Watanabe Sei Makoto
1996

A grove of light-emitting rods sprout from beds of carbon fibre. Undulating surfaces of polished black granite, ceramic tiles and moulded pads lap like waves against hard, white panels, rectangular units raised above the ground. A nest of taut cords cluster like a force field of high-tension wires. Architect Watanabe Sei Makoto's 1996 Carbon Fibre Garden, an adjunct to his K-Museum design, sits incongruously, like the creation of a science fiction writer, at the centre of Odaiba, an artificial island in Tokyo Bay.

Part of an ambitious construction programme known as the Tokyo Waterfront City, the island is home to isolated superstructures, half-finished technological experiments, empty lots, pedestrian bridges and belts of exposed land. Appropriately, the museum and its light-absorbing and reflecting garden, a structure of intended impermanence, add to the sense of otherness.

The vehicular appearance of the museum, cantilevered over the ground like a slightly off-kilter space module, creates a sense of mobility, as if the structure is tilted, poised for take-off. Offsetting the brittle angularity are the wave-like surfaces of the three-dimensional garden, its billowing shape suggestive of the movement of wind and water. As in a Japanese stone garden, each perspective reveals a different combination of interacting elements. The garden, like the island, is a tabula rasa, light and motion defining a design built on reclaimed land without a shred of cultural history, human settlement, nature or identity.

The design, representing the place where architecture and landscape contouring converge, may have been doomed to failure from the outset. It was hardly surprising that the museum's primary exhibits, highlighting the Tokyo Bureau of Port and Harbor's utility system's pipes and electrical conduits, attracted little visitor interest or excitement. A sign outside the fenced-in museum reads 'Temporarily Closed'. Weeds are gaining tentative purchase on the edges of the garden, some of the soft tiles that resemble black bubblewrap have fallen off and the bristling silver rods, 'environmental sculptures' in Watanabe's words, are losing their original lustre. The structure, in fact, is showing early signs of becoming a *hykyo*, a Japanese word for the abandoned theme parks, factories and arcades much beloved of experimental photographers.

Time and merciless exposure to the salt winds are conspiring to obliterate the garden. If the site is not restored and maintained, its barriers removed so that visitors can explore the tactile nature of its materials, erosion will gain the upper hand, turning the installation into a ruin.

1
Soft black tiles and sinuous casing create fluid landscaped surfaces.

1

2

3

2
Resembling bubble wrap, the black tiles have an appealing tactility.

3
Watanabe calls these rods ‘environmental sculptures’.

4
The futuristic design poses the question: is it possible to create a garden from purely manufactured materials?

4

CARBON FIBRE GARDEN

PROJECT

LOCATION

YEAR

Sagawa Art Museum
Moriyama, Shiga
1998

204

The beauty of water has long been appreciated by the Japanese. A millennium ago, Heian-era courtiers enjoyed boating trips, floating across garden ponds on clear, moonlit nights when the constellations were crisp and visible. Drifting on a sheet of reflective water would have created the pleasant illusion of existing between two dark, subtly illuminated zones.

Close to Lake Biwa and the Hiei and Hira mountains, the low, grey, hangar-like, gabled buildings of the Sagawa Art Museum, opened in 1998, blend unobtrusively with their natural surroundings. Dedicated to Japanese painting, ceramics and sculpture, the museum consists of two monochrome structures standing on pillars that appear to float over the shallow surfaces of a water garden.

What defines a garden? Can water replace or rival solid matter like earth and rock? An element of nature is clearly required. In this case, water, one of the most essential components of life, provides that. It is easily replenished by rain and, if manipulated into motion, it is less vulnerable to decay than organic matter. Water's capacity for transformation, its function as a mirror reflecting the sky, clouds and play of light, its immaterial forms as mist and evaporation, have always appealed to Japanese garden designers.

Contemporary tastes favour shallow water and rectilinear containers over the deep, sunken ponds of a previous age. Like infinity pools, the surfaces of the water pools touch the lips of their containers. There are also islands made of compacted earth with spears of bull-rush, reminiscent of the floating vegetable gardens of Dal Lake in Kashmir or Inle Lake in Myanmar.

The confines of the traditional Japanese tearoom, with its muted light, have been freed and replaced with a spacious interior designed by ceramic artist Raku Kichizaemon XV, which is surrounded by broad glass panels looking out onto the water garden and its islands of reeds. The teahouse is approached not in the usual way, via a garden of mossy ground cover, but by stepping stones placed over a sheet of water. A note of abstraction and immateriality is struck in a sunken hall beneath the museum, where an underwater skylight admits a single pillar of water-reflective light that ripples across a wall of untreated concrete.

Instead of rocks, water provides the medium for contemplation, for the attainment of quietude. In Buddhism, water, or its substitutes, sand and gravel, in the dry landscape garden, is allegorical, a symbol of the passage of life and the serenity of the afterworld.

1
Cantilevered over the pond, ceramic artist Raku Kichizaemon XV's modern teahouse.

1

2

2
The elegance and perfect form of water.
3
There is only the slightest space between the surface of the pond and the museum's walkways.
4
Islands of bull-rushes add interest to the flat surface of the pool.

3

4

5

6

5
Tanks of perfectly interlocking water evoke the perfection of infinity pools.

6
Glass tanks reflect sky and water.

7

7
A band of light, a water reflection, in one of the lower galleries.

Okinawan Gardens

If the Japanese looked towards mountains and river valleys as sources in creating the rock arrangements that form the power grids of their gardens, Okinawans cast their eyes over the translucent seas that surround their sub-tropical islands, finding in marine gardens models for landscaping.

The gardens of the once independent Kingdom of Ryukyu, now Japan's southernmost prefecture, reflect horticultural and climatic differences from Japanese landscapes, but also hint at disparities in cultural preferences and taste. Their fabulist rocks, floating pavilions, arched bridges and clusters of banana frond and ripening bamboo are closer to the gardens of retired Chinese administrators in Suzhou than the temple, aristocratic or tea gardens of Kyoto. At first glance, these landscapes appear to be the creation of Chinese sorcerers or Daoist recluses, their forms and saturated patinas the result of countless years of tropical erosion.

The clearest example of a garden closely modelled on Chinese principles, but with strong native elements, is Shikina-en in the prefectural capital of Naha. Faithfully reassembled in the post-war period, the formal grounds of the original garden, completed in 1799, served as a second residence for the royal family and a guest villa for visiting dignitaries from China. The choice of stones, reflecting the Chinese preference for jagged, spiny rocks with pitted surfaces, hollows, cavities and blowholes, reflects a quite different aesthetic from that of Japanese gardens, where surfaces are darker, smoother to the touch and more understated. Though less given to the complexities of metaphysical abstraction or Buddhist iconography, gardens like this do not represent a disintegration of meaning or a rejection of symbolism, but rather an emphasis on the simple delight to be drawn from an appreciation of form and materials.

The combination of rain and sunlight, acting as a photosynthetic fertilizer, creates the variegated greens of gardens whose plantings always seem glossy and lustrous. Plantings include cycads, aspidistra, bird nest ferns, bougainvillea, heliconias, red and yellow hibiscus, lines of typhoon-resistant *fukugi* trees and the ghostly roots of banyan and ficus trees.

Writers and landscape specialists have paid little serious attention to Okinawan gardens. These radiant, sun-lit plots, with their lush sub-tropical flora, have, it seems, little appeal for garden scholars. The omission is perhaps attributable to the perception of Okinawan gardens as either a minor landscape genre or an essentially non-Japanese form.

Shikina-en in Naha is closely modelled on Chinese principles.

PROJECT

Toyota City Museum of Art

LOCATION

Kozakahonmachi, Toyota-City, Aichi Prefecture

DESIGNER

Peter Walker

YEAR

1996

212

Opened in 1995 on the hilltop site of a former castle, today's museum and its landscaped grounds overlook an industrial city. Approached along an entrance drive that twists and turns through woodland, the museum deliberately delays revealing itself.

The first feature visitors see is a large pond with a linear grid of Japanese irises, resembling the serried rows of a rice field. With a lone willow tree and a bubbling fountain, the sheet of water acts as a forecourt to the transparent façades of the museum buildings.

Designed by Taniguchi Yoshio, the architecture effortlessly complements the garden segments created by American landscape designer Peter Walker. Walker is no stranger to Japan. A designer whose portfolio includes cultural gardens, academic campuses, shopping plazas, corporate headquarters and urban regeneration projects, his early ideas, germinating during his days as a student at the Harvard Graduate School of Design, were profoundly influenced by his Japanese tutor Sasaki Hideo. In subsequent years, he collaborated with several Japanese architects, including Isozaki Arata. Reflecting his knowledge of contemporary art as well as cultural and ecological issues, the museum grounds are arranged to provide visitors with a series of stimulating spatial experiences.

Featuring permanent works by the likes of Egon Schiele, Edvard Munch, Constantin Brancusi and Gustav Klimt, the museum's buildings, characterized by huge, light-conducting plate glass windows, take art outside, with Daniel Buren's terrace-level work using surfaces and mirrors to reflect and fuse the garden and architecture. Objects that might have been stone lanterns in a traditional garden have been replaced in the museum's outdoor dry landscape garden with polished black steles. The only exterior view is the sky.

1
Light and open sky play an important part in the design of this garden.

1

TOYOTA CITY MUSEUM OF ART

2

3

2
The forecourt of the museum contains many inventive water features.
3
Open skies and expanses of water characterize the entrance zone to the museum.

4

4-5
Reflective mirrors capture portions of the garden.

5

TOYOTA CITY MUSEUM OF ART

6

6
The traditional dry landscape garden teleported into the modern age.

Imperial Chrysanthemums

One of the most richly connotative blooms of autumn is the chrysanthemum, its sixteen petals the emblem of the Japanese imperial family. Originally cultivated to enrich the gardens of feudal lords, exhibitions of chrysanthemum sculptures were also held in parks and temple grounds. Among the display tables of chrysanthemum bonsai were *kiku-ningyo*, carefully fashioned life-sized dolls representing court ladies and historic figures attired in kimonos.

One of the finest places to view chrysanthemums is Tokyo's old imperial park, Shinjuku Gyoen, where stalls and bamboo pavilions decorated with red and white cloth and purple banners display tiers and vertical beds of flowers trained over frames of supportive wire. A member of the Compositae flower family, there are over 200 varieties of exhibition chrysanthemum in Japan, with in excess of 100 sub-species. The cultivation of the flower by approved growers and their use as a motif was restricted to the imperial household until the middle of the nineteenth century, when its popularity made such bans unenforceable.

The temptation to add symbolism to a flower already imbued with myriad meaning is evident in its association with longevity. The motif of chrysanthemums floating on water is found on kimonos, representing a river endowed with life-extending properties. A form of horticultural geomancy, with the perfect symmetry of its centre standing for a solar wheel, the flower's axis corresponds with the four cardinal points.

A floral representation of the iconic Mount Fuji at the Shinjuku Gyoen Garden in Tokyo.

PROJECT

Hotel Le Port

LOCATION

Kojimachi, Hirakawa-cho, Chiyoda-ku, Tokyo

DESIGNER

Masuno Shunmyo

YEAR

1998

The character of work-driven Tokyo business districts like Kojimachi may mitigate against nature, but at the Hotel Le Port, first- and fourth-floor spaces have been set aside for a momentary refreshing of the senses, for the idea of gardens as spatial interludes.

An ambitious project, an attempt to create the sensation of being within a mountain and forest setting, designer Masuno Shunmyo's three interlinked gardens are together named Seizan-Ryokusui no Niwa, The Garden of Blue Mountains and Green Water. *Seizan* has the additional meaning of Nirvana; *Ryokusui* is an alternative term for nature.

A closer look at rock dispositions reveals a deliberate symbolism that references specific groupings, such as Mount Sumeru (Sumisen in Japanese), the centre of the Buddhist cosmos, and the use of odd numbers, in accord with the Taoist concept of asymmetrical balance. Greenery is provided in the form of moss mounds and beds, mountain maple and the Japanese ash tree.

A distinctive *koetsu-gaki* fence transects the upper courtyard garden. Connoisseurs will recognize that the bamboo fence has associations with its place of origin, Koetsu-ji, a Kyoto temple with a graceful set of teahouses. For the informed, such small allusions add extra layers of meaning and enrichment.

Where contoured gravel serves as a representation of a river in the fourth-floor courtyard garden, the ground-floor area, adjacent to a café, features actual water in the form of a pool and superimposed waterfalls. The terraced cascades present a dynamic contrast of two stones: black South African granite cut into slices like a slate roof, and a brown granite. The interplay between the horizontal and vertical surfaces of the waterfall walls and the set of multi-angled, carved rocks rising above the waterline of the pond, in the manner of mountains surfacing from the sea, creates an image not unlike a Cubist interpretation of the choppy movement of waves across an ocean.

1
The solidity of fortress-like walls contrasts with gently flowing water.

1

2

3

2
The upright stone walls replicate the side of the hotel building itself.

3
Sliced granite emphasizes the directional flow of water.

4
A curving *koetsu-gaki* fence is visible at the rear of the inner garden.

5
An open courtyard garden references a traditional garden form.

4

5

PROJECT

LOCATION

DESIGNER

YEAR

Cerulean Tower Tokyu Hotel
Sakuragaokacho, Shibuya-ku, Tokyo
Masuno Shunmyo
2001

Prominent garden designer and Soto Zen priest Masuno Shunmyo embraces both tradition and modernity in his work, combining a profound grasp of Japanese culture with an artist's perspective on landscape.

Kanzatei, the name of his arresting Cerulean Tower hotel garden, translates as 'The Sitting Peacefully Garden'. The title comes from a Zen expression, *kanza shite shofou o kiku*, meaning to 'sit calmly, listening to the sound in the pines'. The cacophonous traffic sounds outside the garden, and an endless stream of high-spirited pedestrians in one of Tokyo's busiest young fashion and entertainment centres, are muted by the judicious planting of bushes, trees and dense ground cover of moss and dwarf bamboo.

Designed to be viewed from an inside lobby and restaurant area, rock shelves of graduated tones and concentrations, more compressed towards the top, descend to terraces that flatten, then sink into large particles of grey gravel in an effect that evokes a series of tiered waves lapping against the shoreline of the hotel, its glass sea wall. Masuno has left the wedging grooves visible on some of the slabs, deliberately revealing the hand of the mason. The natural forms of the greenery contrast with the chiselled stone and sculpted rock, representing in equal measure the organic and geometric.

Like the most powerful works of art, this Zen-infused design raises more questions than it answers. How to respond to waves of pale granite, primal slabs in the centre of one of the most maddeningly intense visitor districts of the capital? What do everyday customers make of the design? The view, seen through a wide expanse of glass, an experience similar to watching the slow orbiting of exotic sea creatures in an aquarium, surely has an emotional, or magnetic effect on guests. The tables nearest the garden are always the most popular.

1
Split rock adds to the sense of geological frisson.

1

CERULEAN TOWER TOKYU HOTEL

2

3

2
The curving café window matches the contours of the garden's sculpture forms.
3
The designer has left wedging grooves on some of the flat rocks in the garden, a reminder of human intervention.
4
Tiered shelves contrast with the softer plantings of trees and bamboo grass.

4

PROJECT	Zuiganzan Enkou-ji
LOCATION	Sakyou-ku, Kyoto
DESIGNER	Keikan Tsubo
YEAR	2013

It seems that the ancient practice of having rock gardens designed and built by *ishi-tate-so*, stone-setting priests, has not entirely vanished. Just a few steps away from the much-visited hermitage of Shisen-do in a northeastern district of Kyoto, the Rinzai Zen sect temple of Zuiganzan Enkou-ji, despite its exquisite collection of Buddhist artefacts and an ancient statue of a thousand-armed Kannon Bodhisattva, receives few visitors. Autumn is the exception, when people descend on the temple's rear garden, known as Jugyu no Niwa, a woodland with a mossy ground cover transected by a stone path. The word 'jugyu' is analogous with the Buddhist notion of a path to enlightenment, and is another example of how apparently simple forms of naming and terminology act as signage freighted with meaning in Japanese gardens.

The Rinzai sect teaches the art of listening to one's inner voice and seeking truth, an objective it has applied to its gardens, which act as tools for contemplation. In design terms, the endeavour to penetrate the surface of life and nature, to reveal inner truth, results in the scouring of superfluous ornamentation. A preference for the suggestive over the explicit results in pared-back gardens featuring little more than sand, gravel and rock.

Those who enter the temple grounds are greeted by a rather extraordinary Modernist dry landscape garden, known as the Honyutei. The design combines the primitive and abstract by utilizing striking sculptural forms, swirls of upended tile and stone clusters representing a dragon soaring towards the heavens. The temple provides little or no explanation of the garden or its intentions. It is presented as an enigma that can be interpreted, but not solved.

The garden was created in 2013 by Keikan Tsubo and his brother, both Buddhist priests. Keikan claims to have no specialist knowledge of Japanese gardens, insisting that the design was created entirely in the spirit of Buddhism. Formal training or not, it is interesting to find priests today adapting the principles of their medieval stone-setting forebears. Seeking neither fame nor commercial gain, such dedicated aesthetic designers are a rarity.

1
Upended roof tiles add to the effect of gravel, which represents waves and sea currents.

1

2
Swirls of upright tile promote the idea of motion.
3
Granite stepping stones lead visitors through the garden, a rare concession to access in usually restricted stone arrangements.
4 →
A cluster of rocks, representing a soaring dragon, adds drama to the landscape.

2

3

ZUIGANZAN ENKOU-JI

ZUIGANZAN ENKOU-JI

PROJECT	**Hyakudanen**
LOCATION	**Awaji-shi, Hyogo Prefecture**
DESIGNER	**Tadao Ando**
YEAR	**2000**

234

Built near the epicentre of the 1995 Great Hanshin Earthquake, the highlight of architect Ando Tadao's Awaji Yumebutai hotel, conference centre, botanical garden, tea ceremony building, theatre and park complex is the Hyakudanen, or 'One Hundred Stepped Garden', consisting of one hundred concrete-encased flower and shrub beds stacked against the hillside in a pattern that evokes a mathematical grid. The design represents an interesting post-war tendency, where renowned architects have become involved in landscape art.

The original location of the site, a barren plot with its sand and earth removed for massive landfill projects in Osaka Bay, amounted to a vision of nature desecrated. Two hundred and thirty-five staircases run through the complex, making it possible to view each of the units individually. Although the flora within the maze was planted to reflect the four seasons, many of the giant planters are succumbing to neglect, the victims of invasive weeds.

A memorial to those who perished in the earthquake, the site was conceived as 'a symbol of rebirth'. Ando said, 'Yumebutai commemorates death and devastation by celebrating their opposites – life and beauty.'[1] Its descending grid of giant square planters and individualized stairs might, from a distance, be mistaken for a hillside cemetery or the skeleton of an exposed catacomb, but Ando has said that the grounds of the Alhambra Palace in Granada were one of the models for the garden. Specifically, he cited the Islamic landscape's synthesis of flowerbeds and plants and its mastery of water circulation as inspiration.

A free-standing lift and viewing platform provide a 360-degree panorama of the garden, its complex geometry and a ten-metre (33-feet) wide graduated stream, resembling a gentle cascade, that runs through the grounds. The aquatic theme also emerges in Ando's Shell Garden, an adjunct to the main complex, consisting of thousands of scallops manually affixed to the bottom of shallow pools.

Completed in 2000, the project was designed to help heal the wounds between man and nature. One would have to ask if that end has been achieved, or whether the proliferation of exposed, cast-in-place concrete, already discoloured and suffering from surface cracking, compromises nature. To put it differently, is the abundance of concrete antithetical to a garden, or is it the precursor of a new form of landscape art?

1
As weeds take purchase and grassy patches burn out, the garden is showing signs of under-maintenance.

1

2

2
A view across the garden to fishing boats in the Inland Sea.
3
Graduated plant containers slope down towards the sea.

3

HYAKUDANEN

4

4
Thousands of shells form the bed of a shallow pond.
5
Ando employed different construction surfaces for his water garden section.

5

PROJECT
LOCATION
DESIGNER
YEAR

CIAL Tsurumi Station Roof Garden
Tsurumi-ku, Yokohama City
Masuno Shunmyo
2000

The improbability of finding a Japanese landscape garden on the roof of the Japan Rail East Tsurumi Station, with its integrated multi-purpose shopping complex, adds to the Surrealist nature of the encounter.

Before ascending to the roof of the CIAL Tsurumi building, visitors encounter garden signifiers on the fifth and sixth floors, where designer Masuno Shunmyo has placed a number of telling aesthetic and sculptural objects. Placed around the lifts and escalators of the fifth floor, black granite flooring inlaid with stepping stones introduces the theme of rock. At the rear of a large *tokonoma* (alcove) containing a carved stone bench, a calligraphic scroll hangs on a wall covered in handmade, lacquered *washi* paper. Masuno was also responsible for creating a Japanese-themed garden and aesthetic elements for the stylish fifth-floor Zen café Zagetsu Kazuha, which also has a traditional four-and-a-half mat tearoom. Another recessed space greets visitors exiting the sixth-floor lift, where a granite bench fronts a back wall partially covered with a vertical canvas of dark green moss. The garden theme is reiterated within the circulation area around the escalators, in the form of two granite blocks, whose incised circular tops contain carefully arranged plants.

On the roof, a broad expanse of stone and concrete and a wooden deck complement a strip of grassy hillocks and rocks, collectively known as the Seifuen garden. This open area also serves as a children's play zone and events space. Seifuen means 'garden of refreshing breezes', an indicator of its restorative and recreational function.

Adjacent, but a world apart in design and intention, the Zagetsu-tei, a perfectly flat *kanshoshiki teien* contemplation garden, is entirely devoid of greenery. Consisting simply of horizontal and upright rocks and raked pea gravel, the garden is screened off by slated fences. These block out intrusive buildings that might be distractions to meditation and repose, the designer's ultimate aim in our ascent to this rooftop site.

1
Contemporary fencing masks the urban sprawl beyond the roof garden.

1

CIAL TSURUMI STATION ROOF GARDEN

2

3

4

2
Lines of raked gravel add depth of field to what is, essentially, a small garden.
3
Raked and striated gravel provide greater depth of field.
4
Judicious rock placements add interest to this corner of the garden.

5
Foreground garden forms compete with the urban configuration beyond.

6
A more orthodox garden design, but with grass and a wooden deck.

7
Ground plants soften the effect of harder, industrial materials.

5

6

7

CIAL TSURUMI STATION ROOF GARDEN

PROJECT

LOCATION

YEAR

Momijiyama Garden
Sunpu Castle Park, Aoi-ku, Shizuoka
2001

Built in 2001 on the site of a ruined castle kitchen, the Momijiyama Garden is an unapologetic recreation of the Edo-period stroll garden, a return to playfulness and whimsicality with a fresh gloss. A harmonious composition, this tried and tested garden form stands as proof that traditional design and artisanal standards still exist in the modern age.

The grounds are divided into scenic segments, including the Sato no Niwa (Village Garden), the Umi no Niwa (Garden of the Sea) and the Yamazato no Niwa (Garden of the Mountain). Rocks at the centre of the pond represent views along the nearby Izu Peninsula.

The grounds feature familiar stroll garden elements, including cherry and maple trees, stone lanterns, weathered washbasins and millstones, a *suhama* pebble beach and a typical *yatsuhashi* zig-zag bridge, floating above a small iris field. The visual highlight of the garden is a miniature Mount Fuji, encircled by azalea bushes designed to resemble the iconic tea plantations of the Shizuoka region, where the garden is located.

As accessible as a municipal park, the grounds represent a return to the simple pleasures and novelties of the excursion garden, in a contemporary age when designers are striving to be taken more seriously as artists in landscape innovation.

1
Hedges in the form of tea plantations represent a mini-Mount Fuji area landscape.

1

MOMIJIYAMA GARDEN

2

3

2
These swirling hedges resemble tea bushes planted around a miniature Mount Fuji.
3
A miniaturization of a rocky landscape contrasting with tea bushes.
4
An expansive view of the garden from a recently constructed pavilion.

MOMIJIYAMA GARDEN

PROJECT

LOCATION

YEAR

Osaka Station Roof Garden
Umeda Sanchome, Kita-ku, Osaka
2012

The world's first roof gardens are believed to have been built on the Ziggurats of Mesopotamia, from the fourth millennium to 600 BCE, their terraces of hanging vines and flowers creating coolness in the desert climate.

The completion in 2012 of the Osaka Station Roof Garden, elevated above the urban desert of Osaka, achieves a similar, albeit modest effect, by turning a disused, heat-absorbing roof area into a small habitat of water vapour-releasing plants, azalea bushes, pine and cherry trees, a generous ground cover of evergreen *tamaryu* (mondo grass) and sculpted stone forms.

The garden appears to be less an exercise in reducing the heat island effect in cities, however, than an attempt to delight the senses of visitors, reminding them, amid a surge of interest in English-style residential gardens, of their landscape heritage by co-opting older aesthetics in the service of a modern Japanese garden.

Occupying the tenth floor of the station's North Gate Building, the design is known as the Yawaragi-no-niwa, meaning 'peaceful garden'. Living up to its name, the garden creates a sense of well-being for visitors, providing a strolling space for shoppers and customers patronizing the tenth-floor complex of restaurants. It gives them the opportunity to savour the improved air quality and superb views of Osaka from the perspective of a garden suspended above one of Japan's most bustling cities.

1
The garden is divided into two sections: one enhanced by greenery, the other consisting of purely stone.

1

OSAKA STATION ROOF GARDEN

2

2
A skilful synergy of stone, hedge and mondo grass.
3
Careful stone placement promotes depth of field in this small garden.

3

OSAKA STATION ROOF GARDEN

4

5

4
Granite slabs and azaleas frame a lush bed of *tamaryu*, or mondo grass.

5
Ornamental details in a corner of the garden.

PROJECT
LOCATION
DESIGNER
YEAR

Namba Parks
Nambanaka, Naniwa-ku, Osaka
Jon Jerde
2003

256

Unveiled in 2003 on the former site of Osaka Baseball Park, this nine-storey shopping centre and cinema complex is refreshed by multiple rooftop gardens. More a garden in Japan than a Japanese garden, Namba Parks was designed by American architect Jon Jerde (1940–2015) and his company, The Jerde Partnership. Jerde's work focused on experiential venues and the commercial revitalization of under-performing city centres.

Namba Parks is highly representative of the late architect's work, which was known for maximizing sight lines, creating fragmented spaces and introducing features such as parapets, plunging ravine-like openings, serpentine pathways and surfacing structures in arresting, striated colours. The interstices between buildings were of primary importance, freeing up spaces for strolling. In this instance, terraces ascend around a central 'canyon' that resembles a seismic fissure.

Jerde's designs ran the risk of appearing cartoonish, but this may have been intentional. He likened his multi-level shopping centres to the sequencing of acts in a play. Synthetic urban architecture and gardens were conceived as forms of visual entertainment, an experience akin to walking through the lot of a Hollywood movie set. Jerde would make film-like storyboards sketching out the routes, the 'narratives' of visitors. The blocky, multicoloured wonderland of Namba Parks, with its shopping arcades, boutiques, hotels, restaurants and bars, adheres strongly to the idea of architecture serving commercial and entertainment ends.

In a huge undertaking, 300 species of plants and 70,000 trees were planted throughout the open-air sections of the complex. Flowers, groves of trees, shrubs, waterfalls, ponds, rock clusters, miniature lawns and an artificial stream create a bird- and insect-friendly environment far removed from the tumult of Osaka.

Like a tree extending from a narrow trunk, its branches and leaves spreading out, the gardens ascend through eight floors of the complex, with greenery-covered walkways and containing walls. The predominantly concrete, circular eighth-floor amphitheatre, an events space for concerts, is softened by a garden with generous plantings, which, in turn, act as a corridor to the ninth-floor landscape garden.

At Namba Parks, the synthetic appearance of Jerde's structures is softened by greenery. Taking a cue, perhaps, from the shopping centres, highway bridges and grounds of public housing estates in Singapore, where flora is ubiquitous, plantings swarm over the faux geological layering of the floors and open terraces, adding extra drama and vitality.

1
The terraces of Namba Parks bring greenery to the shopping and entertainment experience.

1

2

3

4

2
Visitors can appreciate the complexity of merging gardens and architecture from both inside and outside of Namba Parks.

3
Swathes of greenery are a surprising complement to modern building surfaces.

4
Designer Jon Jerde was known for creating dramatic free spaces between building blocks.

Mira Locher

260 The Role of the Japanese Garden in the Twenty-First Century

1

2

Over their long history, Japanese gardens have transformed to reflect the beliefs and trends of various eras, yet they remain places to enjoy the beauty of nature and spark the imagination. Paradise gardens, featuring artificial hills, streams and ponds with islands and bridges, developed in tandem with Pure Land Buddhism during the Heian era (794–1185). Wealthy aristocrats enjoyed leisure time walking in their gardens but also writing poetry and hosting gatherings. Minimalist *karesansui* meditation gardens developed from the late fourteenth century, simultaneous to the rise of Zen Buddhism and the *bushido* warrior ethic of discipline of the mind and body. During the strictly controlled Edo period (1600–1868), earlier garden styles were refined as well as synthesised in expansive stroll gardens.

With the Japanese government's ambition to quickly Westernize in the late nineteenth century, Japanese gardens became living relics of the past, and Western-style parks and gardens came into vogue. It wasn't until the 1930s that designers began exploring the possibility of the modern Japanese garden. One of the leaders was Shigemori Mirei, a *nihonga* painter, scholar of traditional Japanese culture and self-trained garden designer. Shigemori drew on his vast knowledge of traditional garden design for his novel modern gardens. His designs appear both familiar and new, once again mirroring shifts in society. Shigemori's innovative approach propelled the evolution of Japanese garden design, opening the door for other garden designers, including prolific designer and Zen Buddhist priest Masuno Shunmyo, to expand the aesthetic vocabulary of the Japanese garden. Still, the function of Shigemori's gardens remained familiar – they were primarily for enjoying the beauty of the ever-changing nature and for introspection.

In the twenty-first century, the role of the Japanese garden has transformed once again. Masuno Shunmyo describes gardens as places of self-reflection. While this is not a new function, Masuno stresses the necessity for such tranquil spaces in the present time, with an ever-increasing amount of information available at our fingertips. He emphasizes the need for us to experience the 'abundance of spirit' that can be found in the garden, over the 'abundance of things' that inundate our daily lives.

Related to this is a surge of scientific research into the restorative effect of Japanese gardens. Humankind has long understood the benefit of spending time in nature, and for centuries Japanese gardens have been sites that foster relaxation and contemplation. Led by landscape architect and scholar Goto Seiko and others, research now proves the physiological and psychological reduction of stress through the simple act of viewing a well-designed Japanese garden. While this research is ongoing, it has led to an increase in Japanese gardens being constructed outside of Japan as 'therapeutic landscapes' or 'healing gardens' connected to hospitals and prisons. Examples include the gardens at the Samaritan Lebanon Community Hospital (2004) and the Oregon State Penitentiary (2019), both designed by Kurisu International.

For those unable to visit a Japanese garden, tabletop versions of Japanese rock gardens are available commercially. Numerous websites explain how to create your own, including making a miniature rake to create patterns in sand. If this proves too taxing, computer-generated versions are available. Games like Zen Garden and Niwa allow users to rake sand and place rocks and greenery in different combinations to create their own Japanese-style virtual gardens.

Engaging the mind in another way, Japanese gardens, understood as miniature worlds, are used to illustrate philosophical concepts and encourage action. Irregular garden paths teach the Buddhist concept of mindfulness. The flowing water represented by raked gravel and dry rock waterfalls evokes movement and suggests questions about the nature of time. Diverse materials combined into asymmetrical compositions demonstrate the ability to find unity within diversity. Scholar Julianne Chung suggests Japanese gardens convey both aesthetic and moral reasons for the protection of the natural environment and can inspire people to act as eco-citizens – especially important in a time of climate uncertainty.

1
A carefully framed composition at the Northern Culture Museum garden in Konan-ku, Niigata.

2
Complex, Edo-era landscape design at the Homma Museum of Art garden.

In this vein, concerned that a future disaster might destroy a beloved garden, filmmaker and novelist Shinkai Makoto set his 2013 animated film *The Garden of Words* within Tokyo's Shinjuku Gyoen. Such artistic depictions of Japanese gardens can inspire contemporary readings. Scholars of the Anthropocene Ivo Louro and Ana Matilde Sousa employ the representations of gardens in Miyazaki Hayao's 1997 film *Princess Mononoke* to understand the interdependency of nature and humans within the complex contemporary binary of nature and technoculture, suggesting potential liveable futures on Earth.

Japanese gardens have long sparked the human imagination, leading to innovative ways of understanding the garden's spatial qualities. Enamoured with Japan from his first visit in 1962 and inspired by the spaces defined by the rocks and raked gravel of the Ryoan-ji garden in Kyoto, American composer and visual artist John Cage created a musical score expressing his interpretation of the garden through sound and drawings. Completed in 1985, *Ryoan-ji* emphasizes the harmonious asymmetry and profound substance of the 'empty' space. Cage's modern compositions shocked the musical world, including Japanese composer Takemitsu Toru, who turned to Japanese traditions for inspiration in his own works after a 1964 meeting with Cage. Takemitsu went on to use aesthetic principles from the Japanese garden to create a unique sound experience, exemplified by his 1973 composition *In an Autumn Garden*. Contemporary composers such as Michael Fowler examine the spatial and auditory aspects of Japanese gardens to conceive novel sonic environments, such as Fowler's composition for electronic and live instruments, *Sesshutei as Spatial Model*.

As well as inspiring musical composition, in the twenty-first century the Japanese garden serves as a site for the study of soundscapes. Recent investigations explore varied forms of multisensory interaction, such as the relationship of sound to movement and behaviour. Swedish researcher Gunnar Cerwén uses this analysis to develop 'Soundscape Action' design tools to reduce noise in urban parks and squares, allowing other sounds to be highlighted over traffic noise.

Employing Japanese gardens as tactical means to catalyse and cultivate different ways of spatial and strategic thinking has moved beyond philosophy and the arts. Recent academic explorations utilize the physical traits of the Japanese garden to create virtual gardens representing unrelated concepts. Researchers Yuzawa Hideto and Gloria Mark created a prototype virtual desktop Japanese garden to display workers' tasks for colleagues to see, thereby creating awareness of multitasking as a collaborative activity and reducing unnecessary interruptions.

Similarly connecting the physical world of the Japanese garden to the virtual – and then back to the physical – researchers Yuval Kahlon and Fujii Haruyuki examine typical rock configurations in Japanese gardens as sets of symbolic and spatial relationships that can inform conceptual descriptions or potential meanings within Computer-Aided Design (CAD) frameworks. In a 2020 study they propose that a dry waterfall suggests specific spatial relationships connected to external meaning (such as water and scenery), and the relationship between the configuration and the meaning can inform a concept usable in CAD as a stylistic 'building block'. These building blocks then can be used to create new spatial and metaphorical relationships, perhaps leading to the auto-generation of not-yet-imagined design concepts and forms.

3

The role of the Japanese garden in the twenty-first century continues to expand through contemporary philosophical concepts and scientific studies, particularly regarding wellness and multi-sensory experiences. These explorations and studies suggest future functions that will further enhance our understanding of the Japanese garden – and yet, its important role in the human imagination, for self-reflection and creative inspiration, remains unchanged.

3
Dispensing with nature at the Carbon Fibre Garden on Tokyo's Odaiba Island.

4
Inspired by the sight of a coiled snake on the site, the Spiral Canal, part of the Murou Art Forest in Nara, also resembles a Heian-era winding stream.

PROJECT

LOCATION

YEAR

Abeno Harukas Garden Terrace
Abenosuji, Abeno-ku, Osaka
2014

Terraces in Japan are commonly requisitioned as car parks, AstroTurf fairways, children's amusement parks or to house a small, dedicated Shinto shrine, but this elevated garden terrace serves an altogether different vision, typifying the Japanese garden's preoccupation with hedges, bushes and topiary. In this instance, low hedges are fashioned into geometric blocks, divided by flagstone paths, a horizontal design observed from a standing height, which places the rooftop landscape in the Japanese *hira-niwa*, or flat garden, category.

The custom of pruning bushes, hedges and shrubbery into tight, compressed forms originated from the need to create gardens in confined spaces. Greenery of this kind is an integral component of the garden, complementing the natural landscape, or in this instance, the cityscape beyond its boundaries. The clipped hedge in Japan has been described by writer Marc Peter Keane as an 'architectural element made of garden materials'.[1] The Japanese garden aesthetic favours flowing, organic shapes grown at low levels or in intense groupings, but rather than remaining on an exclusively flat plane, in this garden two rows of tree varietals have been planted to provide verticality.

Unlike referential ornamental elements, such as stone lanterns, miniature pagodas and water basins, bushes are organic matter. Where stone objects benefit from neglect, the moss and lichen that grow on them creating a patina of age that lends them character, topiary, even of the simplest type, does better with careful maintenance. Unless the trimming is done with skill, however, as it is in this terrace setting, the results can look extremely artificial.

There is no sound of insects up here on the sixteenth floor. Instead, we hear the distant hum of the city below, a thrumming soundboard, like a field of electric cicadas in full throat. Currently Japan's tallest skyscraper, the structure is formed from ascending blocks that house brand and souvenir shops, cafés, a hotel, department store, art museum and observation deck, as well as other facilities and amenities, collectively combining the goal of utility and leisure. The complex lives up to its claim to be the 'future of multifunctional urban space in the sky'.

During the winter months, the garden is decorated with illuminations. The name Harukas comes from an old Japanese expression meaning 'to brighten and clarify'. In accord with the idea of enlightened architecture and landscaping, the terrace is the first aerial garden in the city to be bathed with light from the rising sun.

1
The triangular forms of hedge patches promote depth of field.

1

ABENO HARUKAS GARDEN TERRACE

2

3

2
The roof garden after a drenching from rain.
3
The garden offers a restorative rest zone for busy shoppers and office workers.
4
The lush greenery of the garden contrasts with the urban geometry of the cityscape.

PROJECT

Fukuda Art Museum

LOCATION

Ukyo-ku, Arashiyama, Kyoto

DESIGNER

Mitani Yasuhiko

YEAR

2019

Based on an original design by award-winning landscape architect Mitani Yasuhiko, the private Fukuda Art Museum opened in October 2019 in Arashiyama, a scenic location adjacent to the Oi River. Following Mitani's design, Ueyakato Landscape, a long-established Kyoto garden company, undertook the construction.

Water gently cascades from six small elevations into the garden's main feature, its pond, complementing the flow of the Oi River. Stones set above the pond's surface allow a portion of the water to pass through shade, a strategy that helps to decrease its exposure to sunlight and suppress turbidity-generating algae. Narrow stone slabs rising above the waterline mirror the staggered water breaks placed across the nearby Oi River, the garden's 'currents' replicating its downstream energy flows. The stones, placed parallel to the axis of the art museum's main building, form a reflective, horizontal line. The rocks appear to float weightlessly on the surface of the water in a powerful, illusionary act of levitation.

The bottom of the pond is notable for its sunken *ichi-matsu* design, a traditional Japanese chequered form. Similar to a gingham pattern, it represents wealth for descendants, with the repetition of alternating squares signifying prosperity in perpetuity. The pond's long, megalith-like rocks contrast with the softer, organic presence of hydrangeas, maples, yellow irises, ferns and a moss-covered *tsukubai* (water basin) at the edges of the water, components that reference older garden elements. Tree varieties found on the slopes of Mount Arashiyama and Mount Ogura, both visible from the garden and acting as borrowed views, have been used within it. These include cherry, maple and red pines. An internal corridor and café areas allow the changes of the four seasons to be viewed from inside the museum building.

Mitani has worked as a stonemason, an experience that fine-tuned both his manual dexterity and his judgement in rock placement. In common with traditional garden designers, he prioritizes the idea of creating correspondences between garden design and proximate environments. This considered approach means that his designs emerge from a knowledge of ancient garden principles, rather than simplistically applying interchangeable templates. 'The idea,' Mitani explained in a conversation with art scholar Carola Platzek, 'emerges out of an oscillation between dedication and experience, not from a construction which one simply places across a landscape.'[1]

1
A perfect synergy of modern garden design and architecture.

1

2

2
The museum is surrounded by hills, river and garden.
3
A single rock, though static, adds motion and direction.

3

4
Tension and balance are created by facing these rocks in opposite directions.

5
Stone fragments and a mossy shore act as embankments for the pond.

4

5

6
A moss-covered water basin provides a traditional element.
7
A bamboo-covered well head adds interest to the borders of the garden.
8
The highly arranged section of the garden contrasts with the more natural area.

6

7

8

PROJECT

LOCATION

YEAR

Oazo Roof Terrace
Marunouchi, Chiyoda-ku, Tokyo
2004

Opposite Tokyo Station, in the heart of the commercial district of Marunouchi, the Oazo Roof Terrace Garden, a 640-square-metre (6,889-square-foot) plot owned by Mitsubishi Jisho Corporation, could hardly be more central.

In a city where a mere seven percent of land is green space, the advent some decades ago of the roof garden was timely. What could easily have been utilized as a café or lifeless concrete plaza has, in a generous public service gesture, been turned into a small, green haven for shoppers and office workers, trapped in the groves of bleak skyscrapers that typify this important business district. It's no coincidence that the 'oazo' in the name of the Marunouchi Oazo Building is taken from the Esperanto word for 'oasis'.

With an adjacent hotel lobby, the garden is surrounded by offices, whose workers are able to look down on its restorative greenery. Verticality complements horizontal ground cover, the massed greenery intended to help reduce the heat island effect. A horticultural version of civilization and wilderness is evoked in mixed parterres of geometrically precise bushes grown next to Japanese grasses, like aureola and *carex oshimensis*, a rhizomatous evergreen. Two vertical walls of evergreen ferns, with samples like *kujaku shida* (five-finger fern), soften building surfaces and add height to the overall scheme.

1
A portion of wall plays host to a vertical garden.

1

OAZO ROOF TERRACE

2
Greenery provides much needed relief from the surrounding press of concrete and glass.
3
Converging walkways and geometric hedges engage the eye.
4
Placing plant and sculptural forms at different levels creates an effective illusion of space.
5 →
Sculptural objects add form. and interest.

2

3

4

OAZO ROOF TERRACE

5

Irises

An old adage of Japanese gardeners is that when viewing stones with the intention of making a purchase, you should never come to a decision in the rain. Glistening and soaked, they have a dark lustre that perfectly enhances their understated beauty. Custom has it that irises, blooming during Japan's rainy season in mid-June and early July, similarly benefit from a good drenching.

Irises were first cultivated in the capital, a major horticultural centre, by a farmer named Izaemon Kodaka in the 1660s, when he began growing the flower in a marshy plot of land beside the Arakawa River in the village of Horikiri, now squarely within the urban sprawl of east Tokyo. A descendant of Izaemon built a garden there and opened it to the public in the early nineteenth century, a forerunner of the present Horikiri-Shobu-en. Among the visitors to the garden was the great woodblock artist Hiroshige Utagawa, who produced *Horikiri no Hanashobu* ('The Horikiri Iris Garden'), the print appearing in his classic *One Hundred Views of Edo* series. Listed as perennial herbs, its iris beds are descended from Edo-period varieties, a type known as *hanashobu*, or *Iris ensata*, an ornamental water plant that thrives in humus- and acid-rich, moisture-retentive soil. Typically, its flowers are 20 cm (8 inches) in width, either single- or double-petalled, appearing in shades of dark blue, purple, white and pink. A rhizomatous perennial, its erect stems are generally between 60 and 80 cm (24–32 inches) in height. The flower, also known as the Japanese iris, was introduced to Europe in 1839.

A superb representation of the flowers can be seen in Korin Ogata's *Irises*, a double six-fold screen painting in which the flowers are portrayed against a background of gold foil on paper. The screen is displayed at Tokyo's Nezu Museum during the early iris season, when a small batch of the flowers blossom within the institute's Japanese garden.

Earlier examples of the flower can be traced to other parts of the country. A species known as *kakitsubata* (rabbit ear iris) is mentioned in the tenth-century *Tales of Ise*, an anthology of lyrical tales mixed with poems. A character in one of the narratives, Ariwara no Narihira, arriving in the district of Yatsuhashi ('Eight Bridges'), observes the flower from the vantage point of eight bridges crisscrossing a marsh. There is something theatrical about stepping onto the raised planks that zigzag through these irrigated gardens. An exception to species that do well in damp soil conditions is the *ayame* iris. Completing the trio of most common iris types, it actually prefers dry, grassy locations.

A small but glorious eruption of irises, known in Japanese as *hanashobu*, at the Tokyo Imperial Palace Ninomaru Gardens.

PROJECT

Kyushu Sangyo University Campus

LOCATION

Matsukadai, Higashi-ku, Fukuoka

DESIGNER

Design Network

YEAR

2012

On entering the university campus, visitors and students are met by asymmetrical paths, a vast oval pergola, three-legged stools, serpentine concrete and cloud-shaped benches. None of which quite prepares you for the sight of a dazzling structure that initially resembles the contours of a green amphitheatre whose axis has been scrambled.

Like dizzying staircases in a Salvador Dalí painting, a dreamscape of cascading labyrinths, angled concrete planters, containers for earth and grass, descend in beautifully measured geometry. Another comparison would be the graduated squares and rectangles of traditional Japanese rice terraces.

Ancient agricultural structures, the terraces may have been engineering marvels, but they were essentially practical measures to make the best use of limited land in rural areas. The aesthetic appreciation of form came much later, and they are now also valued for the way they reframe the landscape. In Japanese, the terraces are called *tanada*, but are also known more fondly as *mizu-kagami*, or water mirrors, the irrigated pools reflecting sky and clouds. Instead of the *doha*, the broad earthen dikes and rims that support the rural terraces, the university campus design substitutes a number of ascending and descending pathways. Rather than evoke the sense of nostalgia associated with rural terraces, the intention of the design is to revitalize an existing campus.

Created by Fukuoka-based landscaping company Design Network, the campus is intended to provide students with relaxing spaces. Sections fit together with the precision of bolted panels found in ultra-modern constructions. Taking advantage of elevation changes within the campus environment, the design team have created a rich topography of straight, curved and irregular lines and diverse rhythmic patterns that visitors can walk through or linger in. The designers, whose objective was for students to pass through the grounds with minimal stress, have written that they wanted to create a 'landscape that encourages both the flow of people and their stagnation in certain places, as well as the interaction of those two patterns'.[1]

Exploring this geometric puzzle, we realize that there is no single composition, that every vantage point reveals a unique angle and framing. The sheer visual enjoyment obviates the search for definition, reminding us that ultimately, the question of whether the topography represents a garden or landscape art is irrelevant.

1
The angled greenery is intended to refresh students as they approach the university's main buildings.

1

KYUSHU SANGYO UNIVERSITY CAMPUS

2

2
The graduated landscape stages resemble Japanese rice fields.
3
The terraces can also be viewed from inside the main building.
4
Every perspective on the design reveals a different pairing of angles.

3

4

PROJECT

Art Biotop Water Garden

LOCATION

Nasu-machi, Nasu-gun, Tochigi Prefecture

DESIGNER

Ishigami Junya

YEAR

2018

A highly successful fusion of technological ingenuity and natural elements takes place in architect Ishigami Junya's 2018 Water Garden at Art Biotop, in the highlands of Tochigi Prefecture. Aside from being a work of outstanding originality and beauty, it is a fine example of the contemporary merging of indigenous garden thinking with natural and adjusted landforms.

Located on the site of a former meadow and a rice field, with forested perimeters hosting dense beds of moss, the garden's agricultural history seeps into the present. Here we see a forest of deciduous trees, transplanted maples, cherry, beech, Korean hornbeams and *Quercus serratas*, standing among a series of artificial ponds or basins, called biotops. Water is replenished from a nearby river, utilizing the time-honoured floodgate technique to adjust the water levels of rice fields. Invisible pipes circulate the water back into the river, reflecting the notion of life resembling the flow of water. Aside from their aesthetic appeal, the ponds serve as miniature habitats for aquatic plants, water insects and reptiles. Fallen foliage is allowed to decompose at the bottom of the ponds, enriching the site with nutrients. Moss, transplanted into the interstices between trees and water, adds to the intense but subdued greenery. Winner of the Obel Award, an international architectural prize given to projects that offer 'seminal solutions to urgent problems', the garden is designed to recalibrate mind and body, providing a space for meditative dialogues between nature and observer. With the design mechanics carefully concealed beneath the surface of the site, one experiences a sensation akin to stumbling upon an entirely natural scene. Blurring the lines between architecture, environmentalism and art, Ishigami's earthwork landscape and garden is both a model of geometric complexity and order, and an evolving, organic ecosystem.

This duality of vision will evoke images such as rice paddies and the ancient scenery of *satoyama*, the areas between cultivated, arable land and forested hillsides, a rural ideal that has come, with some nostalgia attached, to stand for the ideal of symbiotic co-existence between humankind and nature.

Ultimately, the garden, in the words of the Obel Prize jury, is both a highly artificial landscape and an 'undeniably natural and living organism that grows and changes by its own inherent dynamics'.

1
Circular rain ripples mirror the shape of the pools.

1

2

3

2
The designer hints at tradition in placing a small stone bridge across one of the pools.
3
Once inside the water forest, time stands still.
4
Tree islands are placed in many of the pools.

4

289

5

5
A path of stepping stones, possibly sourced from old gardens.

6
The water garden at its best, some say, during a light rainfall.

6

When We Talk About Zen

The over-application of the term Zen to describe everything from interior designs to restaurant menus pored over by celebrities and fashionistas, taking in expressions like a 'Zen moment', can be misleading.

The practice, along with certain Japanese garden forms associated with it, has not, despite the efforts of early disseminators, writers and analysts, such as Suzuki Shunryu, Ruth Fuller Sasaki and Alan Watts, been widely understood outside of Japan. For many people, Zen has come to simply denote minimalism.

True Zen is no easy thing. It is often conducted in draughty winter halls that are poorly ventilated in hot Japanese summers, or on hard wooden decks overlooking so-called Zen gardens. As your body is being assailed by pain and discomfort, you are inveighed to disengage from the bone chills and muscular knots and ascend to a higher state.

Comprehending Zen, even achieving a small purchase on its steep rock face, can feel overwhelming, like trying to name every plant, flower and tree on the planet, a work of improbable scale, beyond the scope of a single life. Perhaps that is why Buddhism offers the hope of an infinite number of existences.

Raked patterns on the sand mounds at Henen-in, a temple in Kyoto.

PROJECT

Yokoo Tadanori House Garden

LOCATION

Teshima Island, Tonosho-cho, Kagawa Prefecture

DESIGNER

Tadanori Yokoo

YEAR

2013

Teshima, a tiny island in the Seto Inland Sea, would seem an improbable setting for a collaboration between international artist Tadanori Yokoo and architect Nagayama Yuko.

Active since the 1960s, Tadanori, a prolific graphic designer, printmaker, illustrator, stage set designer and figurative artist, has appropriated ideas from the Expressionist and Surrealist movements, forging a style that mixes pastiche and sixties psychedelia. His interest in science fiction, spiritualism, comic art, woodblock printing and Japanese aesthetics permeates his creations, many of which seek to overcome nostalgia through dark, satirical humour and allegory.

The renovated and repurposed Yokoo Tadanori House Garden opened in 2013. Initial reactions from visitors are mixed. Some will be spellbound, others repelled at its apparent sullying of tradition. The occasional visitor will burst into hysterical laughter. No one will be indifferent. This is, no doubt, deliberate on Tadanori's part, as he is known for blurring the line between innovation and hoax.

An exercise in counter-intuitive aesthetics, a number of ornamental objects – among them, a plastic crane, a turtle and blue and yellow mosaic tiles, items easily picked up in the discount sections of garden centres – add to the curiosity, or effrontery, felt by the viewer. In creating this disturbing, but iridescent work, Tadanori has deconstructed the Japanese garden and reassembled it in his own iconoclastic, colour-saturated private vision of landscape art.

Tadanori's early Pop Art style follows, as writer Donald Richie put it, 'a hard-edged cartoon line in bright kindergarten colors'.[1] It is, indeed, almost as if a class of toddlers has been let loose with brushes and pots of lurid, primary paints. In this landscape Tadanori's retro Pop vocabulary, however, extends beyond paint to the materials and composition itself. Look closely at the rock dispositions, alignments and spacing, and we see that the artist has a surprisingly sophisticated grasp of Japanese garden design.

In common with contemporary art in general, the work poses more questions than it answers. In his high-kitsch design, is Tadanori ridiculing the Japanese garden, as he did in canvases depicting icons like Mount Fuji, the Rising Sun flag and kamikaze pilots, or is he revering it? Are we gazing at a toxic interpretation of the Japanese garden, or an anarchic masterpiece?

If the purpose of the modern garden is to unsettle us, to up-end our assumptions, it succeeds brilliantly.

1
Traditional clay and tile walls surrounding a controversial garden design.

1

YOKOO TADANORI HOUSE GARDEN

2

2
Tadanori's use of lurid colours and tile creates a kind of anti-garden.

3
A plastic turtle seems anomalous to garden purists.

4
Tadanori has placed natural rocks against painted ones.

3

4

PROJECT	**The Wall of Hope**
LOCATION	**Oyodonaka, Kita-ku, Osaka**
DESIGNER	**Ando Tadao**
YEAR	**2013**

Osaka-born architect and Pritzker Prize winner Ando Tadao's name is more frequently associated with unfinished concrete structures than greenery, but his ambitious *Kibo-no-Kabe* (Wall of Hope) garden assembly, unveiled in 2013, was part of a mission to make Osaka a greener city.

A fiercely independent, self-taught architect, Ando nevertheless aligns himself with the school of Japanese design known as Critical Regionalism, a movement that takes pains to consider the local culture and environment of a proposed plot before plans are conceived, construction begun.

Located within the Shin-Umeda urban complex, at the foot of the soaring Umeda Sky Building, the Wall of Hope reflects the public, collective nature of Ando's more recent work, involving design concepts aimed at achieving harmony between architecture and nature. The site-specific project conforms with his insistence that structures should allow for the random movement and penetration of light and wind. In this context, Ando has spoken about 'void spaces', with elements like doors and windows transcending their primary function and allowing light to enter, or, in the most experimental instances, sculpt space.

Stainless steel cages and nets, forming a 9-metre/30-foot high, 78-metre/256-foot long and 3-metre/10-foot deep structure, act as metal planters, supporting more than one hundred luxuriant flowers, shrubs and assorted greenery. Adjacent to the Wall, the banks and bed of a meandering stream made from tile host a number of polished structures, suggestive of the stones requisitioned from rivers and mountains that are used in more traditional Japanese gardens.

Conceived in collaboration with local businesses, in the hope that it can help transform Osaka into a greener city, the garden has been praised as a 'new model for urban greening and nature restoration'.[1] There is no standard measure for judging the success of such projects, but it does represent a fresh and creative way to introduce greenery into cities, a template that is likely, in space-pinched urban centres in Japan, to be replicated.

1
A stone sculpture replicates the curving lines of the water course.

1

2

3

4

2
The soaring Umeda Sky Building places the garden firmly in the urban area of Osaka.

3
The Wall of Hope.

4
Construction work is visible through one of the wall's portals.

5

6

5
A channel of gridded tiles adjacent to the wall.
6
Pieces of sculpture add interest to the water channel.
7
A sinuous water channel with marble art objects.

7

PROJECT	**Ginza Six Rooftop Garden**
LOCATION	**Ginza, Chuo-ku, Tokyo**
DESIGNER	**Taniguchi Yoshio**
YEAR	**2017**

302

The short but politically and creatively liberating Taisho era (1912–26) witnessed the debut of the Japanese department store, an innovative, multi-purpose enterprise that, aside from conventional shopping, offered recreational and cultural amenities, such as restaurants, cafés and art galleries. In the post-war period, rooftops would be co-opted as children's amusement parks, beer gardens or even mini putting greens. Propitiating the gods of commerce, no department store rooftop was complete without a small Shinto shrine.

A large-scale, luxury-brand commercial facility designed by architect Taniguchi Yoshio, creator of the redesigned Museum of Modern Art in New York, Ginza Six was unveiled in 2017. Covering a generous 4,000 square metres (43,056 square feet) characterized by dense greenery and vegetal walls, the rooftop garden site is divided into grass, woodland, water and promenade zones.

A small grove of cherry trees in the northern section of the roof and a clump of maples in the southern part were planted to reflect Edo-period garden culture. Flowers were chosen for their seasonality, the plants for their perennial durability.

In a contemporary interpretation of the stroll garden, a circulating pathway runs along the periphery of the building, offering varying viewpoints of downtown Tokyo. The glass walls around the edges reflect vignettes of the Tokyo skyline. The Zen concept of the dynamic void is a difficult sell in urban Japan, the empty space of the plaza occasionally co-opted as a DJ stage or for theatrical performances, the water mirror used in the winter as a skating rink.

Then, just when you thought the Ginza Six garden might have gone entirely secular, you turn a corner and the red *tori* gate of a miniature Shinto shrine appears.

1
Connecting corridors sustain the roof terrace's green theme.

1

GINZA SIX ROOFTOP GARDEN

2
The long, open outer passages provide glimpses of the city centre.

2

GINZA SIX ROOFTOP GARDEN

3

3
Exposed tiers of plantings, placed outside to catch the rain.

4
The shallow pool is also popular with young children as a paddling area.

5
A leafy arbour at the heart of the busy Ginza shopping district.

4

5

PROJECT

LOCATION

DESIGNER

YEAR

Shinsho-ji Zen Museum and Gardens
Numakuma-cho, Fukuyama
Kohei Nawa
2016

Surrounded by farmland and forest, the Rinzai Zen temple of Shinsho-ji stands in extensive grounds replete with teahouses, meditation halls, a museum dedicated to the work of the monk-artist Hakuin, an udon restaurant and a wooden bathhouse – all features intended to make the transition to its principal gardens an initiation into aspects of Japanese culture.

Created in 2016 by sculptor Kohei Nawa and his creative platform Sandwich, Kohtei, a large vessel-shaped structure, supported on pillars that act as framing devices for viewing the surrounding landscape, serves as an art pavilion and installation space. Its surfaces, made from planks and thousands of shingles made of Japanese cypress applied to thin tiles affixed with bamboo nails, form a roof over much of the dry landscape garden. In another gesture fusing tradition and modernity, the shingles were laid by Kyoto-based roofers specializing in 300-year-old techniques.

The team's stated objective was to create a monolithic piece of architecture 'that floats on waves surrounded by mountains and is themed to work with three fundamental materials: wood, stone and water'. They wanted the experience of standing underneath such a space to enhance 'the stark materiality of the landscape against the airy contours of the wooden roof'.[1] The designers of the garden invite visitors to experience the spirit of Zen by strolling through the landscapes and engaging with mind- and body-cleansing activities, such as contemplating a piece of Zen calligraphy, receiving instruction in the hand-copying of sutras or partaking in a bowl of powdered green tea.

The temple's traditional pond and mountain garden shares its grounds with the startlingly modern landscape under the hall. One would expect the natural rocks in the Japanese garden to clash with the contemporary garden, but the traditional placement of stones complements vast beds of *warikuri-ishi*, broken, locally quarried and cut rocks. Instead of opposition, we have counterpart. To the initially bewildered visitor, schooled in more orthodox design values, the dissected appearance of the rock beds may look more like debris in the aftermath of a quarry detonation or earthquake than a garden.

Both gardens, however, share a common vitality, one from the rampant growth of nature that needs constant maintenance, the other from a harsh aridity that forces us to see a powerful sculptural dynamic made visible.

1
A surface of *warikuri-ishi* cut rocks.

1

2

3

4 

2
Sealed granite steps contrast with looser stone arrangements.
3
The stone garden is sheltered beneath the Kohtei, an art pavilion.
4
A bridge to the mysterious Kohtei art installation structure.
5 →
A modern art object embedded in quarried rocks.

PROJECT

Hoshinoya Kyoto

LOCATION

Arashiyama, Genrokuzan-cho, Nishikyo-ku, Kyoto

DESIGNER

Hasegawa Hiroki

YEAR

2009

Guests arrive at Hoshinoya Kyoto, an exclusive *ryokan* (Japanese inn), after boarding a private boat from a quay close to Arashiyama's graceful Togetsu-kyo Bridge.

The inn is located in an area of Kyoto that has some of the city's strictest landscape regulations, which created an exciting challenge to make a modern garden that would complement its environs. The garden was designed by Hasegawa Hiroki, head of Studio Onsite, and constructed by the long-established Kyoto firm Ueyakato Landscape. The entrance to this green compound consists of patterned flagstones sourced from the Kyoto area, but also sites in the Hyogo, Yamanashi, Okayama and Kagawa regions. Before guests arrive, the stones are watered, a traditional welcome greeting at teahouses.

Built on an excavated ledge above the Oi River, at a sufficient remove from the seething tourism of Arashiyama, Hoshinoya Kyoto blends seamlessly into a supremely quiet natural setting, on a site that was once part of a residential retreat owned by Heian-era nobility. Although Kyoto is often perceived as a repository of traditional culture, it has a strong avant-garde character, priding itself on innovation. Accordingly, the grounds of Hoshinoya Kyoto fuse time-tested garden principles with a contemporary sensibility.

The Oku-no-niwa, or Inner Garden, a modern interpretation of the dry landscape garden, consisting of contoured, smoked roof tiles and white sand suggestive of water currents or raked gravel, can be entered, a rarity in such designs. The top surfaces of the larger rocks have been flattened and polished, transforming them into horizontal mirrors that reflect the changing seasonal colours of the trees. The *shakkei*, or borrowed views, consisting of the far bank of the river and forested slopes, are entirely natural.

So deep and secluded is its location that this secret garden, invisible from the outside, but with an extensive view of the surrounding nature and river topography from its interior, succeeds, without apparent contradiction, in introducing modern design elements into an environment that is singularly elemental.

1
Moss is used discreetly throughout the garden.

1

2

2
The upright tiles suggest raked gravel and water currents.
3
Moss thrives in the shaded, humid depths of this wooded area.
4
The designer has chosen to use flat-topped rocks to promote a horizontal plain.

3

4

PROJECT

LOCATION

DESIGNER

YEAR

Enoura Observatory
Enoura, Odawara, Kanagawa Prefecture
Sugimoto Hiroshi
2017

Built across ten acres (four hectares) of rocky hillside overlooking Sagami Bay, the Enoura Observatory sits on a steep ledge with views towards the ocean horizon.

Part of the Kataura district of Odawara City, Enoura Observatory might be classified as a multi-disciplinary cultural project, one that includes gardens, a gallery, a teahouse, pavilions, a shrine and an optical glass stage. Like the gardens, each of the structures requisitions traditional Japanese building styles and methods. Twenty years in the planning and construction, the observatory opened in 2017. More additions are planned.

A drystone wall, providing a backdrop to the 100-metre (328-foot) gallery and its collection of Modernist sculptures, symbolically links ancient and contemporary garden design. The wall is made from Oya stone, a distinctively porous, pitted rock with a pleasing patina that changes as it ages and weathers. The structure is angled so that on the morning of the summer solstice, rays of light travel along its full inner length. In common with other buildings erected throughout the stone gardens, the architecture corresponds to forms built in ancient periods for the observation of the constellations.

During the stone placement for each individual landscape, its creator, Sugimoto Hiroshi, frequently consulted Toshitsuna Tachibana's eleventh-century garden manual *Sakutei-ki*, with its admonition to 'obey the request of the stone'. Favouring horizontal placements, he spent decades collecting unique rocks and stone objects, some unearthed at archaeological sites dating back to the Kofun era (250–592).

Sugimoto, whose work embraces lecturing, solo exhibitions of photography, installation art, architecture, writing projects and theatre productions, has written of his 'archaeoastronomical structures' being created in preparation for the possible collapse of civilization. 'I am making a garden,' he asserts, 'that will devolve beautifully into ruins of stone.'[1]

With the Enoura Observatory project, Sugimoto has created an assemblage filled not with dust and rubble, the inert debris of time, but with enduring stone mysteries for the future to puzzle over. The designer has gone on record saying this is his final work, his legacy.

1
A stone garden arrangement in the form of an astrological clock.

1

2

2
The stone wall side of the main, sea-facing gallery.
3
A deeply fissured rock hints at the ever-present danger of earthquakes in this region.
4
The Modernist main gallery of the complex.
5 →
The complex's impressively located optical glass stage.

3

4

6

6
The observatory grounds offer stunning views of land and sea.

Honourable Visitors

Since the Greek-Irish writer Lafcadio Hearn (1850–1904) and British architect Josiah Conder (1852–1920) published their early accounts of Japanese gardens, there has been a steady stream of notable visitors with special interests in the subject.

Loraine Kuck (1894–1977) authored several influential books on the topic. Other celebrated visitors who left memorable impressions of the gardens they saw include Sacheverell Sitwell (1897–1988), who visited Kyoto in 1958. Sitwell, a descendant of the Plantagenets, expressed unbridled admiration for the city's gardens, which he viewed as superior to European examples. He noted an 'art form developed over a very long period of time ... the great works of little masters'.[1]

Nouveau réalisme artist Yves Klein (1928–1962) visited in 1953, followed by German-American architect Walter Gropius (1883–1969) in 1954. The normally acerbic Peter Quennell (1905–1993), a British writer and literary historian, travelled through Japan in 1931, finding the gardens in Tokyo and Kyoto representative of 'a race of artistic giants'.[2]

Devoting himself in the early 1950s to learning as much as possible about Japanese premodern art and design, Japanese-American sculptor Noguchi Isamu (1904–1988) worked with Japanese architects, designers and artists to develop new ways of reformulating prototypes for the contemporary age. Noguchi had much to say on the subject, writing, 'The art of stone in a Japanese garden is that of placement. Its ideal does not deviate from that of nature.'[3]

As a devoted student of Zen, the composer John Cage (1912–1992) was drawn to the dry landscape form. His abstract score for *Ryoanji*, a composition involving variable instruments and voice, evolved from notes and drawings of the iconic garden. Eschewing conventional musical notation, the movements within *Ryoanji* are played in chance-determined sequences based on the perception of the garden and its fifteen stones as a pre-existing form of musical score.

American artist Richard Serra visited Japan in the 1970s, positing the idea that the layout of the gardens he viewed were 'based on the perceptual principles of time, meditation and motion'.[4] British painter David Hockney used over 130 layered Polaroid images for his photo montage *Walking in the Zen Garden, Ryoanji Temple*. He sought to make sense of its perfect rectangular form and asymmetrical content by dismantling and reassembling it. You can see the artist's feet, one sock red and the other brown, moving gingerly along the viewing deck.

'Moss Garden', a track from David Bowie's album *Heroes*, was inspired by Saiho-ji, a Japanese garden in Kyoto, but Shoden-ji, an exquisite, little-visited dry landscape design in northwest Kyoto, was the site he repeatedly returned to. What impressions the musician formed are unknown. Like the gardens, he remained silent on the subject.

Yves Klein in a garden in Kyoto, 1953.

PROJECT	# Aoyama Wall
LOCATION	Emergence Aoyama Complex, Minami-Aoyama, Minato-ku, Tokyo
DESIGNER	Patrick Blanc
YEAR	2011

You might feel you are facing an intensely planted rock shelf or a sheer cliff in a jungle in Sarawak, rather than the backdrop to the counter of a high-end fruit cocktail bar in Tokyo's cool Aoyama district.

As a student, French botanist Patrick Blanc, creator of the vertical garden, studied the life of plants in their natural habitats, particularly life forms that grow at low light levels, in the rainforest understorey, on rock crevices, on tree trunks, in the entrances to caves and on soil-less slopes bereft of water.

Where conventional gardens and parks create green spaces at a calculated remove from buildings, Blanc's work attempts to blur the line between landscaping and architecture by integrating nature and urbanism in a verdant, enjoined space. An advocate for more green spaces and better air quality in cities, Blanc's creations are small-scale models of biodiversity in the urban setting, designed to be a corrective to the disconnect between people and plants. These mini ecosystems have been described as 'botanical tapestries'.[1]

Vertical gardens, particularly of the indoor variety, are usually composed of a metal frame with layers of polyamide felt and PVC affixed to free-standing walls. A closed-circuit system, valve-controlled pipes funnel mineral-rich nutrient solution to the roots of the plants, encouraging them to flouish. Any excess water is re-inserted into the pipes.

All of this is carefully concealed at Aoyama Wall, its green canvas ingeniously supporting monstera, philodendron, climbing fig, herbaceous plantings, mosses and various species of fern. Some of the Japanese fern varietals planted here include holly fern, royal and ostrich ferns, hart's tongue fern and, from the southern climes of Okinawa, the bird nest fern.

1
Plantings and moss create rich gradations of greenery.

1

AOYAMA WALL

2
Spirits and glasses waiting for customers.

2

AOYAMA WALL

PROJECT
LOCATION
DESIGNER
YEAR

Genji Kyoto
Hashidono-cho, Shimogyo-ku, Kyoto
Marc Peter Keane
2022

One of the most exciting fusions of contemporary garden design and architecture, the master plan of two non-Japanese professionals was unveiled at the Genji Kyoto boutique hotel in the spring of 2022. Located in a local neighbourhood beside the Kamogawa River, the hotel gardens were created by Kyoto-based landscape designer and garden scholar Marc Peter Keane, the building by architect Geoffrey P. Moussas.

Each guest room has either its own *tsubo niwa*, a dedicated pocket garden, or a rustic stone object associated with garden ornamentation and symbolism. The stone works are fine examples of the practice of *mitate mono*, in which found objects are requisitioned and repurposed. In one room, a *mizo*, a hand-carved granite gutter once used in an old factory, has been transformed into a decorative garden element. In another, an egg-shaped stone, formerly used as a water basin, has been turned upwards, becoming an imposing sculptural component of the garden.

The central garden next to the lobby is called the Ukifune Garden. The name is taken from a chapter at the very end of *The Tale of Genji*, an early eleventh-century narrative, considered to be the world's first novel. In the account, a young woman, the eponymous Ukifune, is buffeted by the winds of life and love, caught between two powerful urges towards two different men. *Ukifune*, meaning 'a boat adrift', is a metaphor used in a poem that appears in that chapter to express the evanescence of life. The large stone in the garden, with a topping of moss, also represents planet Earth. The vessel-shaped stone floats upon a bed of stones, a *kare nagare*, or dry winding stream, symbolizing the fragile passage of life. An almost voltaic energy emanates from the stream, with its tightly braided stones flowing beneath a small bridge that conveys guests to the hotel lifts. 'In our Ukifune Garden,' Keane notes, 'a single boat-like stone captures that image, but also extends the reference beyond the *Tale of Genji* to suggest that our Earth itself is also a drifting boat of sorts, carrying its ephemeral cargo of life through the galaxy.'[1]

Superimposing traditional effects on contemporary materials, Moussas has requisitioned an ancient Japanese technique known as *sugi ita katawaku*, in which the fossil-like impressions of cedar boards are left on interior and exterior concrete walling, creating a sense of warmth. In this way, with its rich web of references, the hotel structure becomes a work of art, a series of garden galleries and viewing points in which guests participate and interact.

1
A powerful concentration of upright stones promotes the idea of motion and flow.

1

2

3

2
One of the guest rooms' small *tsubo niwa* (inner garden).

3
The Modernist entrance to the Genji Kyoto.

4
The rock in the upper section of the river represents a drifting boat.

4

GENJI KYOTO

Stephen Mansfield

334 Visions and Prospects

1

2

Does the liberal, permissive spirit that prevails today in Japanese garden design imply a severing of connections to the aesthetic tastes and values of the past, or a recalibration? Is it feasible to completely reject the past, to dispense with the mooring blocks of tradition? Is it possible for fresh traditions to stem from modernity?

Contemporary gardens read like message boards for the near future. Substituting for hills and mountains, high-rise buildings are already treated as borrowed scenery; rooftop garden designers, conscious of weight issues, are resorting to hollowing out natural rocks, or replacing them with fibreglass equivalents. The existence of roof and graduated gardens prefigures the construction of more vertical gardens in space-squeezed Japanese cities. Like major works of architecture, gardens are site-specific, but the idea of dismantling and reassembling highly regarded gardens in the manner of mobile homes may become a viable alternative to demolition.

With more freedom to explore the autonomous structure of gardens, the rules of composition and framing, and the complex symbolic and narrative allusions implicit in older gardens, will be far less circumscribed. Such ultra-modern creations, however, run the risk of falling prey to the snares of stylistic obsolescence, to Jean Cocteau's adage that 'to be up-to-date is to be quickly out-of-date'.[1]

Japan shows little reservation about tearing down historical structures. An act synonymous in other parts of the world with cultural vandalism, the evisceration of the past in Japan is aided by a collusive form of collective amnesia. While society is fixated on the present, material history is reduced to memory landscapes. A stone garden on a rooftop or high-rise in New York or Paris, where structures are built for the ages, will likely outlast their Japanese equivalents. Nothing, of course, can hold back the advance of time in the garden. Today's dry landscape grids, potent mindscapes formed from powerful arrangements of rock, eventually turn to gardens of sand and dust. Acceptance of such processes is partly traceable to the concept of *fueki ryuko*, the complementary nature of stability and change, the term deriving from the Buddhist idea of the eternally flowing, the ability to adapt and submit to current imperatives. Swayed more by the objectives of contemporary art and sculpture, gardens of the near future, rather than attempting to halt the passage of time, will be willingly swept along by it.

Though not the main concern of this book, pseudo-English gardens, by far the most popular residential type, are indicators of altered tastes and cultural reorientation. Stone lanterns, pagodas and washbasins, bamboo fences and plantings of juniper, podocarp, maple, azalea and cycad have been usurped by the personal tastes of garden owners, which include garden gnomes, pots of begonia, hanging baskets of pansies and iron rose trellises. As the Christmas season approaches, many neighbourhood gardens are festooned with fairy lights and models of reindeer. What could have possessed people to extirpate the time-honoured landscapes that once existed in suburban Japan, in favour of these fantasias of ersatz ornamentation? Part of it may be connected to the contemporary preference for brilliance and whimsy, the radiant over the subdued, which can be traced to the immediate post-war period, a dismal time remembered for its ruined cities, food shortages and dysfunctional services. One stirring mantra from this period was *akarui seikatsu*, a life full of light. In the new aesthetic order, shadows, side lighting and intermediate tones were banished, memories of the war subjected to eviscerating rays from new forms of illumination.

The shift from private to civic space, from the exclusive to the public and accessible, has inevitably led to commercialization. If visitors to gardens today complain about the imperative to generate revenue from selling trinkets in souvenir stalls, serving powdered green tea and confectionery in arbours and pavilions, the occasional markets set up in the entrance grounds of gardens and the requisitioning of garden space for open-air wedding receptions overseen by Shinto priests and shrine maidens, it should be noted that, historically, quite lavish receptions were once laid on for visiting dignitaries.

1
A contemporary dry landscape garden in the atrium of a corporate building in Tokyo's Marunouchi business district.
2
This water garden on Naoshima Island also serves as a public foot bath.

These events appear to have had an unabashedly mercantile incentive. Records are surprisingly detailed; for example, on a visit in 1701 to Rikugi-en, a large stroll garden in northwest Tokyo, by Keshoin, mother of the fifth Tokugawa shogun, Tsunayoshi, the large entourage of consorts, ladies-in-waiting, footmen, children and retainers, including a priest and physician, were treated to an unstinting generosity that included trays of sweets, sake and fruit, but also inveighed to shop at stalls proffering papier-mâché dolls, fans, flowers, toys and illustrated books. One might compare the event to a fête held by Tsunayoshi's European contemporary, Louis XIV, which involved plays, ballets, a cavalry parade and a banquet stretching over eight days.

It is no coincidence that medieval infirmaries in Europe were attached to cloister gardens that cultivated curative plants and herbs. Beyond the purely aesthetic, Japanese gardens are increasingly valued as sources of well-being. Cherished for their supernal quiet and calm, stone gardens in particular are returning to an older function as instruments for meditation. For the contemporary urban dweller, Japanese gardens provide a counterbalance to the negative forces generated by modern life. Leaving neurosis behind at the garden gate, we feel an almost immediate sense of well-being as we compose or banish our thoughts, enjoying the sensation of entering into alignment with nature and our inner selves. Japanese gardens have their own currents and energy flows, which have healing and regenerative functions. According to Zen, human energy and power are at their optimum when we attain a condition of composed calm and equipoise.

The flow of organic time within the Japanese garden is quite different from the coursing of work or social time. The deceleration that takes place produces a state that makes us calm but aware, relaxed but mindful, tranquil but alert. Our time within the parameters of these mind sanctuaries may be constrained, but is enough to reenergize us, clear out the static from our ears, reflect mindfully on the moment. In accord with Shinto high priest Kaji Kenji's belief that 'the highest commandment of Japanese gardening is not to lose contact with nature, but to connect with it',[2] gardens will play an increasingly important role in achieving the ideal of cities co-existing with nature.

A keen interest in the potential of the modern garden to connect us with both the past and the future bodes well for a fresh regeneration spurred by specialists and gifted enthusiasts with the vision to advance the form into a new age of experimentation.

3
Contemporary gardens are appearing in the most unexpected locations, in this case, a motorway service area.

4
Tiles and coloured stones made from synthetic materials nevertheless evoke traditional design and garden patterns.

Notes and Sources

INTRODUCTION

[1] Tange Kenzo, 'The Secret of the Rock' in *This is Japan*, Tokyo, c. 1962
[2] 'Of Gardens', 1625, in Francis Bacon, *Essays, Civil and Moral*, 'Harvard Classics', New York: P. F. Collier & Son, 1909–14
[3] Yoshinobu Yoshinaga, *Japanese Traditional Gardens*, Tokyo: The Shokokusha Publishing Co, Inc., 1958
[4] Yagasaki Zentaro, unidentified source
[5] Ito Teiji, *The Gardens of Japan*, Tokyo, New York, London: Kodansha International, 1984
[6] Sahei Tokudaiji, quoted in Shirahata Yozaburo, *Daimyo Gardens*, Kyoto: International Research Center for Japanese Studies, 2016. Original source: *Korakuen kiji*
[7] Donald Richie, 'The "Real" Disneyland', in *A Lateral View: Essays on Contemporary Japan*, Tokyo: The Japan Times, 1985
[8] Keijiro Ozawa, 1915, quoted in Shirahata Yozaburo, *Daimyo Gardens*, Kyoto: International Research Center for Japanese Studies, 2016

PART 1
GARDENS OF THE ENTREPRENEURS

[1] Ogawa Jihei, unidentified source
[2] Alex Kerr and Kathy Arlyn Sokol, *Another Kyoto*, Tokyo: Sekai Bunka Publishing Inc., 2016

PART 1
GARDENS OF THE ENTREPRENEURS
PROFILES

MURIN-AN
[1] Loraine Kuck, *The World of the Japanese Garden*, Boston, MA: Weatherhill, 1968

KIUN KAKU
[1] Itoh Teiji, *The Gardens of Japan*, Tokyo, New York, London: Kodansha International, 1984

INTERNATIONAL HOUSE OF JAPAN
[1] *Ueji no niwa – Ogawa Jihei no sekai*, Kyoto: Tankosha, 1990

PART 2
THE MODERN MINDSCAPE

[1] Christian Tschumi, *Mirei Shigemori: Modernizing the Japanese Garden*, Berkeley, CA: Stone Bridge Press, 2005
[2] Shigemori Mitsuaki, *Shigemori Mirei Part 11: The Artistic Universe of Stone Gardens*, Kyoto: Tsushinsha Press, 2010
[3] Shigemori Mirei, *Niwa, Kokoro to Katachi* ('Japanese Gardens: Spirituality and Form'), Japanese only, 1968
[4] Oguni Syuichi in conversation with Carola Platzek, published in Carola Platzek, *Teachings of the Garden: Conversations in Japan*, Schlebrugge, 2020
[5] Yasumoro Sadao and Joseph Cali, *Inside Your Japanese Garden: A Guide to Creating a Unique Garden for Your Home*, North Clarendon, VT: Tuttle Publishing, 2021
[6] Masuno Shunmyo, quoted in Mira Locher, *Zen Garden Design: Mindful Spaces by Shunmyo Masuno, Japan's Leading Garden Designer*, North Clarendon, VT: Tuttle Publishing, 2020
[7] Masuno Shunmyo, 'Reworking Utopia: Contemporary Japanese Garden Design', interview by Stephen Mansfield in *The Japan Times*, 22 May 2022
[8] Humphry Repton, unidentified source

PART 2
THE MODERN MINDSCAPE
PROFILES

SHIGEMORI MIREI GARDEN MUSEUM
[1] Shigemori Mirei, *Niwa, Kokoro to Katachi* ('Japanese Gardens: Spirituality and Form'), Japanese only, 1968

KOZEN-JI
[1] Christian Tschumi, *Mirei Shigemori: Modernizing the Japanese Garden*, Berkeley, CA: Stone Bridge Press, 2005

SEKIZO-JI
[1] Christian Tschumi, *Mirei Shigemori: Modernizing the Japanese Garden*, Berkeley, CA: Stone Bridge Press, 2005

FUKUCHI-IN
[1] Christian Tschumi, *Mirei Shigemori: Modernizing the Japanese Garden*, Berkeley, CA: Stone Bridge Press, 2005

SHONANDAI CULTURAL CENTER
[1] Alison Main and Newell Platten, *The Lure of The Japanese Garden*,

Cambridge, MA: Wakefield Press, 2002
[2] Unidentified source
[3] Hasegawa Itsuko, unidentified source

CANADIAN EMBASSY
[1] Masuno Shunmyo, 'Reworking Utopia: Contemporary Japanese Garden Design', interview by Stephen Mansfield in *The Japan Times*, 22 May 2022

NATIONAL INSTITUTE FOR MATERIALS SCIENCE
[1] Soseki Muso, *Dialogues in a Dream*, Wisdom Publications, 2015

HYAKUDANEN
[1] www.gcoportal.com/tadao-ando-the-hundred-step-garden-at-awaji-yume

ABENO HARUKAS GARDEN TERRACE
[1] Marc Peter Keane, unidentified source

FUKUDA ART MUSEUM
[1] Mitani Yasuhiko in conversation with Carola Platzek, published in Carola Platzek, *Teachings of the Garden: Conversations in Japan*, Schlebrugge, 2020

KYUSHU SANGYO UNIVERSITY CAMPUS
[1] www.world-architects.com/en/architecture-news/reviews/kyushu-sangyo-university-landscape-design, December 2013

YOKOO TADANORI HOUSE GARDEN
[1] Essay on Yokoo Tadanori in Donald Richie, *Partial Views: Essays on Contemporary Japan*, Tokyo: The Japan Times, 1995

THE WALL OF HOPE
[1] Unidentified source

SHINSHO-JI ZEN MUSEUM AND GARDENS
[1] www.archdaily.com

ENOURA OBSERVATORY
[1] Sugimoto Hiroshi, 'A Complex for the End of Time', *The New York Times*, 7 December 2021

AOYAMA WALL
[1] https://journal.illuminatedperfume.com/2012/02/botanical-tapestry.html?m=0

GENJI KYOTO
[1] https://genjikyoto.com/en/gardens

THE ROLE OF JAPANESE GARDENS IN THE TWENTY-FIRST CENTURY

Gunnar Cerwén, 'Listening to Japanese Gardens II: Expanding the Soundscape Action Design Tool', *Journal of Urban Design*, 2020, vol. 25, no. 5, pp. 607–28

Julianne Chung, 'Moral Cultivation: Japanese Gardens, Personal Ideals, and Ecological Citizenship', *The Journal of Aesthetics and Art Criticism*, Autumn 2018, vol. 76, no. 4, pp. 507–18

Michael D. Fowler, *Sound Worlds of Japanese Gardens: An Interdisciplinary Approach to Spatial Thinking*, 1st ed., Transcript Verlag, 2014. http://www.jstor.org/stable/j.ctv371ck8m

Seiko Goto, Yuki Morota, Congcong Liu, Minkai Sun, Bertram Emil Shi and Karl Herrup, 'The Mechanism of Relaxation of Viewing a Japanese Garden: A Pilot Study', *Health Environments Research & Design Journal*, 2020, vol. 13, no. 4, pp. 31–43

Yuval Kahlon and Haruyuki Fujii, 'A Framework for Concept Formation in CAD Systems: A Case Study of Japanese Rock Garden Design', *Computer-Aided Design & Applications*, 2020, vol. 17, no. 2, pp. 419–28

Ivo Louro and Ana Matilde Sousa, 'Nature-Technoculture Binary and the Search for a Safe Operating Space in Hayao Miyazaki's *Mononoke Hime*', in Maria Paula Diogo, Ana Duarte Rodrigues, Ana Simões, Davide Scarso (eds), *Gardens and Human Agency in the Anthropocene*, London: Routledge, 2019, pp. 216–34

Shunmyo Masuno, 'Tomoike no Design no Gaiyō' [Summary of *Coexistent Design*], unpublished essay, trans. Mira Locher, 2012

Hideto Yuzawa and Gloria Mark, 'The Japanese Garden: Task Awareness for Collaborative Multitasking', *Proceedings of the 2010 ACM International Conference on Supporting Group Work*, 2010, Association for Computing Machinery, pp. 253–62

VISIONS & PROSPECTS

[1] Jean Cocteau, unidentified source
[2] Kaji Kenji in conversation with Carola Platzek, published in Carola Platzek, *Teachings of the Garden: Conversations in Japan*, Schlebrugge, 2020

INTERLUDES

THE AESTHETIC LEXICON
[1] Suzuki Daisetz, *Zen and Japanese Culture*, North Clarendon, VT: Tuttle Publishing, 1988

CHERRY BLOSSOMS
[1] Norinaga Motoori, untitled Japanese *waka*, 1791

RYOAN-JI
[1] Shigemori Mirei quoted in Yamada Shoji, *Shots in the Dark: Japan, Zen and the West*, Chicago, IL: University of Chicago Press, 2009
[2] Donald Richie, *Partial Views: Essays on Contemporary Japan*, Tokyo: The Japan Times, 1995

HONOURABLE VISITORS
[1] Sacheverell Sitwell, *The Bridge of the Brocade Sash*, Cleveland, OH: The World Publishing Company, 1959
[2] Peter Quennell, *A Superficial Journey Through Tokyo and Peking*, London: Faber & Faber, 1932
[3] Noguchi Isamu, 'To Intrude on Nature's Way', 1971, reproduced in the Noguchi Museum catalogue
[4] 'Richard Serra discusses Myoshin-ji, Kyoto' (video), June 2020, Fergus McCaffrey Gallery

HISTORICAL PERIODS

Jomon:	10,000–300 BCE
Yayoi:	300 BCE–300 CE
Asuka:	552–710
Nara:	710–794
Heian:	794–1185
Kamakura:	1185–1333
Muromachi:	1336–1573
Momoyama:	1568–1600
Edo:	1600–1868
Meiji:	1868–1912
Taisho:	1912–1926
Showa:	1926–1989
Hesei:	1989–2019
Reiwa:	2019–

Designer Profiles

SOSEKI MUSO (1275–1351)
A renowned Buddhist monk, poet and calligrapher, Soseki is one of Japan's earliest known garden designers. Along with other commissions that survive today, Soseki was responsible for remodelling the immensely important Tenryu-ji temple garden in Arashiyama, and Kyoto's Saiho-ji temple moss garden.

TOYO SESSHU (1420–1506)
A Zen monk, scholar and important Japanese ink landscape painter, only a handful of Sesshu's gardens remain today, but enough to place him at the forefront of a unique approach to landscape design that often replicated the forms seen in his paintings.

ENSHU KOBORI (1579–1647)
An accomplished tea master, Enshu created an original aesthetic known as *kirei sabi*, a bright, refined version of the tea ceremony. As a landscape designer, he is known for his mastery of space and his ability to integrate architecture and gardens. He is also celebrated for his innovative, dynamic forms of topiary.

OGAWA JIHEI (1860–1933)
Working mostly in the Kansai region, Ogawa, combining elements of Western naturalism and traditional Japanese garden aesthetics associated with the refined tastes of Kyoto, is regarded as a pioneer of modern landscaping. He is a master at water management, and his shallow, pebble-strewn streams contrast with powerful waterfall arrangements, the differing aquatic flows creating a natural soundtrack to his gardens.

SHIGEMORI MIREI (1896–1975)
Trained in flower arranging, painting and the tea ceremony, Shigemori transformed himself from aesthetic polyglot to the foremost modern garden designer of his age. Combining extensive research into traditional garden design with fresh avant-garde works that redefined the meaning of Japanese landscaping, Shigemori was both an exciting and contentious figure in the post-war era.

TANGE KENZO (1913–2005)
Japan's first winner of the prestigious Pritzker Prize in architecture, Tange's 1958 landscape design for the Kagawa Prefectural Government Hall combined elements of modernism with the idea of managed nature, cutting and shaping large granite rocks and boulders into forms resembling sculpture. Tange worked on projects with the renowned Japanese-American sculptor and landscape designer Noguchi Isamu.

NAKANE KINSAKU (1917–1995)
A student of urban planning, Nakane became one of the most prominent post-war landscape designers after making a relatively late start with his first design at the age of thirty-eight. Studying architecture may have influenced his insistence on creating meticulously detailed garden design plans before a single rock was set. Adopting a design approach rooted in traditional Japanese garden principles, with an emphasis on naturalism and asymmetry, Nakane was flexible in adapting his ideas to modern sensibilities and contemporary landscaping.

OTANI SACHIO (1924–2013)
Believing that even urban architecture is viewed from the perspective of a naturalistic frame, Otani created intermediary garden spaces as auditoriums for viewing ambient and distant nature. Referencing the Japanese phrase *teioku ichinyo*, meaning the harmonizing of nature and buildings, Otani promoted the idea of co-existence between architecture and landscaping by incorporating traditional garden techniques like *shakkei*, or 'borrowed scenery'.

PETER WALKER (1932–)
As a landscape architect, Walker's long career stretches from work on miniature gardens to city planning. His designs for public parks, corporate headquarters, museums, university campuses and what he has termed 'cultural gardens' are driven by strong environmental considerations. Founder of the journal *Landscape Forum*, and co-author of *Invisible Gardens* (1994), Walker has influenced landscape design through his writing.

TADANORI YOKOO (1936–)
Graphic designer, illustrator, painter and multi-media dabbler Tadanori, the enfant terrible of Japanese visual arts, has created decades of work that has been described as anarchic, chaotic, emotive and deeply autobiographical. Tadanori generates his own magnetic field, one engineered to shock, unsettle and induce feelings of deep discomfort and confusion. All, of course, in the name of art.

JON JERDE (1940–2015)
Aside from individual architectural projects, the American designer's company, The Jerde Partnership, was also tasked with urban planning, regeneration and commercial developments. Jerde's inventive solutions to space limitations resulted in the creation of shopping malls, public plazas and multi-purpose projects like Canal City Hakata in Fukuoka and Tokyo's Roppongi Hills that, because of their multi-level stepped planning, open zones and internal flows, created the illusion of vastness. Jerde's avowed aim was both aesthetic and commercial, to create communal experiences aimed as much at stimulating visitors as inducing them to spend.

HASEGAWA ITSUKO (1941–)
A multiple prize-winning architect, Hasegawa's work is distinguished by the way she views design and landscaping as a public rather than bureaucratic process. Among a handful of prominent women architects in Japan, she is known as an innovator in the use of materials like punched metal and polycarbonate skins. The instinctual character of her public works projects was captured in a statement in which she expressed a wish to 'create a landscape filled with a new form of nature where devices enable one to hear the strange music of the universe'.

ANDO TADAO (1941–)
A former boxer, self-taught architect Ando, a Pritzker Prize winner, works primarily in exposed cast-in-place concrete. Despite the apparent bleakness of his materials, his approach to space utility promotes the circulation of light and air in open, often empty structural zones that follow the contouring of the ambient landscaping, rather than imposing oppositional forms and lines.

MITANI YASUHIKO (1947–)
Drawing from extensive research into the history of Japanese gardens, combined with onsite work in both Japan and abroad, Mitani plays close attention to environmental conditions when designing gardens. His highly contemporary architectural structures, whether hotels or museums, are designed according to traditional principles, which allow for a natural synergy between interior and exterior, between the inner cores of buildings and gardens.

SUGIMOTO HIROSHI (1948–)
Architect, photographer and landscape designer Sugimoto is the ultimate creative multi-tasker. Sugimoto set up the Odawara Art Foundation in 2009, its multidisciplinary arts complex completed in 2016. Sugimoto's photography, installations, garden and architectural designs can be viewed at his Hiroshi Sugimoto Gallery: Time Corridors on Naoshima Island. Never one to do things by halves, Sugimoto's self-declared aim is to explore consciousness, the nature of time and human existence.

WATANABE SEI MAKOTO (1952–)
Author of *Induction Design* (2002), Tokyo-based Watanabe was an early innovator in the use of computers and mathematics as tools in creating his designs. As a manifesto in digest of his approach to architecture and landscaping, Watanabe has written, 'The purpose is not to discover form. The purpose is to discover ways of making cities and architecture that provide better solutions to problems facing the world while at the same time offering greater freedom to the imagination.'

MASUNO SHUNMYO (1953–)
Often described as Japan's leading garden designer, Masuno also happens to be a Soto Zen priest, strongly linking his work to the early 'stone setting priests' who created dry landscape masterpieces. Masuno describes his gardens as spiritual sites in which the mind dwells. His designs combine a deep respect for the teachings of the past with a restless search for originality and the conviction that Japanese gardens are powerful works of art.

PATRICK BLANC (1953–)
As a student, French botanist Patrick Blanc, creator of the vertical garden, studied the life of plants in their natural habitats, particularly life forms that grow at low light levels in the rainforest understorey, on rock crevices, tree trunks, the entrances to caves and soil-less slopes bereft of water. An advocate for more green spaces and better air generation in cities, and gardens as a corrective to the disconnect between people and plants, Blanc's creations, like his Aoyama Wall project in Tokyo, *Mur Végétal* in French, are small-scale models of biodiversity in the urban setting. These mini-ecosystems have been described as 'botanical tapestries'.

MARC PETER KEANE (1958–)
American landscape architect and writer Keane is also a fellow of the Research Center for Japanese Garden Art in Kyoto, his current home base. A designer of gardens for companies, private residences and religious institutes, one of his most recent projects was the design for a private courtyard at Honen-in, a temple in Kyoto. The premise for the garden was the kinetic character of nature, illustrated by the carbon cycle, a reusable system in which carbon atoms pass from the atmosphere into organisms, then exit back into the air. In Keane's visualization of this process, charcoal sticks were embedded in a shallow trench, forming a curved line, winding through a bed of off-white gravel.

ISHIGAMI JUNYA (1974–)
Whether he is designing a flowing slate roof for London's Serpentine Pavilion, the sunken glass corridors of a visitor centre in the Netherlands or a one-kilometre (0.6-mile) long museum on a lake in China, Ishigami has a keen eye for contouring and landscape. Known for his experimental, eco-conscious designs, Ishigami has expressed the importance of creating fresh, transitional spaces between existing environments, what he defines as an 'intermediate condition between nature and human-made elements'.

Glossary of Garden Plants, Trees and Flowers

PLANTS

Sarcandra glabra
ARDISIA TREE
[Senryo]
An evergreen with red berries; often placed at home entrances as a welcome to visitors.

Rhododendron
AZALEA
[Tsutsuji]
A hugely popular bush, with numerous cultivars, that blossoms in April and May.

Phyllostachys edulis
BAMBOO
[Take]
Countless varietals of this evergreen shrub, which is often mistaken for a tree.

Asplenium nidus
BIRD'S NEST FERN
[Ko tani watari]
Native to the warmer parts of Japan, such as southern Kyushu and Okinawa, the fern is sometimes grown in stone basins.

Lespedeza bicolor
BUSH CLOVER
[Hagi]
A deciduous shrub. One of the Seven Flowers of Autumn.

Camellia japonica
CAMELLIA
[Tsubaki]
An evergreen shrub with countless cultivars.

Aspidistra elatior
CAST-IRON PLANT
[Ha ran]
A ground level rhizomatous evergreen with large, dark, fleshy leaves.

Hibiscus mutabilis
COTTON ROSE
[Fuyou]
A flowering shrub, the plant has been grown in Japan since the Muromachi era.

Cycas revoluta
CYCAD, JAPANESE SAGO PALM
[Sotetsu]
A species of gymnosperm used as an ornamental plant.

Anundinaria veitchii
DWARF BAMBOO
[Kuma zasa]
Commonly used as garden ground cover, or grown alongside rocks and stone pathways.

Fatsia japonica
JAPANESE FATSIA
[Yatsude]
A glossy, evergreen shrub.

Haconechloa macra
JAPANESE FOREST GRASS
[Uraha gusa]
A rhizomatous perennial planted beside garden paths and beside rocks.

Ilex crenata
JAPANESE HOLLY
[Inutsuge]
An evergreen shrub native to Japan and East Asia.

Equisetum hyemale
JAPANESE ROUGH HORSETAIL
[Tokusa]
An evergreen perennial herb, resembling rush, often planted alongside ponds and streams, and with moss.

Dryopteris erythrosora
JAPANESE SHIELD FERN
[Benishida]
A native fern, often planted beside garden rocks.

Miscanthus sinensis
JAPANESE SILVER GRASS
[Susuki]
A blue-green-leaved, deciduous grass.

Nelumbo nucifera
LOTUS
[Hasu]
Often grown in gardens and in pots in temples, a glaucous perennial that blossoms in the early morning hours of high summer.

Bryophyta
MOSS
[Koke]
Used as an aesthetically appealing ground cover, there are approximately 1,800 moss species in Japan, 552 in Kyoto alone.

Paeonia suffruticosa
PEONY
[Botan]
A deciduous bush with a red, pink, white and purple flowering.

Dicranopteris
SCRAMBLING FERN
[Koshida]
Suggestive of a forest floor, this fern is often grown in tea gardens and small courtyard gardens.

Daphne odora
WINTER DAPHNE
[Jinchoge]
A fragrant, evergreen shrub.

TREES

Prunus serrulata
CHERRY TREE
[Sakura]
Japan's national flower. With a large number of species, the tree has several botanical names.

Lagerstroemia indica
CREPE MYRTLE
[Sarusuberi]
The dark pink and white flowers of this deciduous tree are associated with the summer months.

Osmanthus fragrans
FRAGRANT OLIVE
[Kin-mokusei]
Dark, glossy leaves. A strong autumn fragrance from clusters of orange flowers.

Ginkgo biloba
GINKGO
[Icho]
A deciduous tree with brilliant yellow autumn leaves.

Chamaecyparis obtusa
HINOKI CYPRESS
[Hinoki]
Evergreen coniferous tree.

Myrica rubra
JAPANESE BAYBERRY
[Yama momo]
A evergreen with dark, glossy leaves, commonly seen in Japanese gardens as a tree or hedge.

Pinus thunbergii
JAPANESE BLACK PINE
[Kuro matsu]
Evergreen conifer with dark bark and oblong cones.

Cryptomeria japonica
JAPANESE CEDAR
[Sugi]
An evergreen coniferous tree.

Tsuga sieboldii
JAPANESE HEMLOCK
[Tsuga]
A tall, conical evergreen conifer, treated as decorative topiary in gardens.

Acer palmatum
JAPANESE MAPLE
[Momiji]
Native deciduous tree.

Diospyros kaki
JAPANESE PERSIMMON
[Kaki]
Fruit trees, like this deciduous varietal with dioecious flowers, occasionally appear in gardens, particularly if they are seasonal or literary indicators.

Ligustrum japonicum
JAPANESE PRIVET
[Nezumi-mochi]
A tree species that is often grown as a shrub or hedge.

Pinus densiflora
JAPANESE RED PINE
[Akamatsu]
An evergreen coniferous tree with a red-brown bark.

Podocarpus macrophyllus
PODOCARP
[Maki]
An evergreen tree, used extensively as a garden hedge.

Prunus mume
PLUM TREE
[Ume]
Its fragrant pink, red and white blossoms flower in winter. There are dedicated plum gardens.

FLOWERS

Chrysanthemum morifolium
CHRYSANTHEMUM
[Kiku]
A vibrant early autumn flower of Chinese origin.

Hydrangea macrophylla
HYDRANGEA
[Ajisai]
A shrub-like rainy-season flower, its blossoming clusters appear in numerous colours, such as blue, white, pink and purple.

Platycodon grandiflorus
JAPANESE BELL FLOWER
[Kikyo]
Also known as the Chinese bell flower, this is a violet-blue herbaceous perennial that blossoms in the summer.

Iris ensata
JAPANESE WATER IRIS
[Hana shobu]
An early summer flower.

Wisteria floribunda
JAPANESE WISTERIA
[Fuji]
A deciduous vine, grown on tall trellises. Lavender and white flowering racemes.

Ipomoea nil
MORNING GLORY
[Asagao]
An energetic summer vine, often displayed in gardens during the summer.

About the Authors

Stephen Mansfield is a British writer, photographer and longtime Japan resident, whose work has appeared in over seventy magazines, newspapers and journals worldwide. Subjects have included travel, interviews, cultural and literary themes. He is a regular contributor to *Nikkei Asia*. He has had twenty books published, and is the author and photographer of four books on Japanese gardens. His work has been translated into several languages, including French, German, Polish and Chinese.

Pico Iyer is the author of seventeen books, translated into twenty-three languages. Three of them describe his life in Japan over the past thirty-seven years: *The Lady and the Monk*, *Autumn Light* and *A Beginner's Guide to Japan*.

Kengo Kuma is one of Japan's leading architects. He is widely known as a prolific writer and philosopher and has designed many notable buildings in Japan and around the world.

Mira Locher joined the University of Manitoba as Dean of the Faculty of Architecture in 2021. She is an educator, author and practising architect.

Shunmyo Masuno is the head priest of a 450-year-old Zen Buddhist temple in Japan, and the country's pre-eminent Zen garden designer.

Tim Richardson is the former landscape editor at *Wallpaper**, gardens editor at *Country Life* and founding editor of *New Eden*. He is the author of numerous books on landscape design.

Acknowledgments

Rather than the work of a single writer or photographer, books like this are the result of tightly coordinated teamwork. In this respect, I have been very fortunate. I would like, firstly, to extend a big thanks to Lucas Dietrich, who green-lighted the project, and to senior editor Helen Fanthorpe, who skilfully steered it to completion. I would also like to thank the highly professional staff who worked on the production of the book, and the design team, led in this instance by Callin Mackintosh. The four guest essayists, Kengo Kuma, Mira Locher, Masuno Shunmyo and Tim Richardson, should be acknowledged for their original, informed contributions.

We were exceedingly fortunate in getting a writer I have long admired, Pico Iyer, to contribute an astute, beautifully framed foreword. A huge thanks to all the landscape designers I contacted, and to the garden administrative staff who made themselves available to me when on site. I would like to thank my wife, Kazuko, for untangling some of the more arcane Japanese language issues relating to names and the historical legacies and provenance of the older gardens. Lastly, an enormous thanks to my son, Rupert, for assisting me in obtaining garden design plans.

Index

Page numbers in *italics* refer to illustrations

On the front cover: Rinsho-ji temple garden.
On the back cover: Fukuoka Sangyo University campus garden.

First published in the United Kingdom in 2025 by Thames & Hudson Ltd, 6–24 Britannia Street, London WC1X 9JD

North American edition published by Timber Press 2025

Timber Press is an imprint of Workman Publishing, a division of Hachette Book Group, Inc. The Timber Press name and logo are registered trademarks of Hachette Book Group, Inc.

Timber Press
Workman Publishing
Hachette Book Group, Inc.
1290 Avenue of the Americas
New York, New York 10104
timberpress.com

p. 82 above: Photo Kiichi Noro/Tokachi Millennium Forest
p. 82 below: Photo Aya Kawachi
p. 325: All rights reserved © The Estate of Yves Klein c/o ADAGP, Paris

Designed by Callin Mackintosh

A catalog record for this book is available from the Library of Congress.

ISBN 978-1-64326-575-9

Printed in China by RR Donnelley